MYTH AMERICA

Can You Imagine
WORDS BY
HARRY PEASE
MUSIC BY
FRED MAYO &
ED. NELSON

MYTH AMERICA

PICTURING WOMEN 1865-1945

BY CAROL WALD

TEXT BY JUDITH PAPACHRISTOU

Book design by Paul Gamarello

Pantheon Books

A Division of Random House, New York

All rights reserved under International and Pan-American
Copyright Conventions. Published in the United States
by Pantheon Books, a division of Random House, Inc.,
New York, and simultaneously in Canada by Random
House of Canada Limited, Toronto.

Library of Congress Cataloging in Publication Data

Wald, Carol.
Myth America: Picturing Women, 1865-1945.

1. Women — United States — History — Pictorial works.
2. Women — United States — Social conditions — Pictorial
works. I. Title.
HQ1419.W28   301.41′2′0973   75-10364
ISBN O-394-49840-2
ISBN O-394-73089-5 pbk.

Manufactured in the United States of America

First Edition

PERMISSIONS ACKNOWLEDGMENTS

Grateful acknowledgment is made to the following for permission to reprint the following copyrighted material: Arrow Company: Advertisement for Arrow Dress Shirts. Painting by Hans Flato. Used by permission. Frank L. Banyai: "The Rose of No Man's Land," sheet-music cover, 2nd verse and chorus. Copyright ©1918 by Leo Feist, Inc. Belwin-Mills Publishing Corp.: I CANNOT BEAR TO SAY GOODBYE Copyright 1918 by Mills Music, Inc. Copyright renewed. Used with permission. All rights reserved. JUST A BABY'S PRAYER AT TWILIGHT Copyright 1918 by Mills Music, Inc. Copyright renewed. Used with permission. All rights reserved. WHEN I SEE YOU I SEE RED, WHITE AND BLUE Copyright 1917 by Mills Music, Inc. Copyright renewed. Used with permission. All rights reserved. Best Foods, CPC International Inc.: Advertisment for Mazola. Copyright 1921. Used by permission. Brown & Bigelow: Two Earl Moran illustrations reproduced by permission of and copyright by Brown & Bigelow, a Division of Standard Packaging, Saint Paul, Minn. The Coca-Cola Company: Two advertisements for Coca-Cola: "Your Thirst Takes Wings," copyright 1941, The Coca-Cola Company; "Christmas Together...Have a Coke," copyright 1945, The Coca-Cola Company. Used by permission. Colgate-Palmolive Company: Six advertisements for Palmolive. Copyright 1921, 1922, 1924, 1928 by the Palmolive Company. Used by permission. Downe Publishing, Inc.: Three covers painted by Harrison Fisher. Copyright 1911, renewed 1939; copyright 1912, renewed 1940; copyright 1914, renewed 1942 by Downe Publishing, Inc.; and for "The Maxfield Parrish Dining Room," painted by J. Duncan Gleason, copyright 1912, renewed 1940 by Downe Publishing, Inc. Reprinted with the permission of Ladies' Home Journal. Eastman Kodak Company: Two advertisements for Kodak. Used with permission. Fuller Brush Company: Advertisment for Fuller Brushes. Copyright 1924 by the F. B. Co. Used by permission. General Mills, Inc.: Two advertisements for Gold Medal Flour which appeared in Ladies' Home Journal. Copyright 1906 and 1912 by Washburn-Crosby Co. Reproduced with the permission of General Mills, Inc. Heinz U.S.A.: Advertisement for H. J. Heinz Company. Copyright 1923 by H.J.H. Co. Used by permission. Judge: One cover. Used by permission. Liggett & Myers Incorporated: Eight old Chesterfield Brand advertisements: "Learn Real Mildness...It's Easy," copyright 1940 by Liggett & Myers Tobacco Co.; "Mr. and Mrs. and Chesterfields," copyright 1938 by Liggett & Myers Tobacco Co.; "A Roundup of All You Want in a Cigarette," copyright 1940 by Liggett & Myers Tobacco Co.; "The Way to More Smoking Pleasure," copyright 1940 by Liggett & Myers Tobacco Co.; "They Rate the Best," copyright 1942 by Liggett & Myers Tobacco Co.; "First Choice, Chesterfield," copyright 1943 by Liggett & Myers Tobacco Co.; "A Glorious Combination," copyright 1939 by Liggett & Myers Tobacco Co.; "They Deliver More Pleasure," copyright 1942 by Liggett & Myers Tobacco Co. Permission granted by Liggett & Myers Incorporated to use each of the above reproductions. All Rights Reserved. Edwin H. Morris and Co., Inc.: "A Mother's Prayer for Her Boy Out There," sheet-music cover. Copyright © 1918 by the Joe Morris Music Co. "America Here's My Boy," sheet-music cover. Copyright © 1917 by the Joe Morris Music Co. Reprinted by permission of Edwin H. Morris & Co., Inc. Nabisco, Inc.: Three CREAM OF WHEAT Cereal advertisements; "Don't Forget Cream of Wheat," copyright 1910 by Cream of Wheat Co., painted by W.V. Cahill; "The Cooking Lesson," copyright 1911 by Cream of Wheat Co., painted by W. V. Cahill; "None But the Brave Deserve the Fare," copyright 1918 by Cream of Wheat Co., painted by Edw. V. Brewer. Printed with permission of Nabisco, Inc. National Canners Association: Advertisement for National Canners Association. Copyright 1921, N.C.A. Used by permission. National Woman's Christian Temperance Union: "The Home vs. the Saloon," postcard. Copyright 1910 by National Woman's Christian Temperance Union. Used by permission. Old Life Magazine: Three covers of old Life Magazine. Used by permission. Oneida Ltd. Silversmiths: Four advertisements for Community Silverplate. Copyright 1927, Oneida Community Ltd., and 1941, Oneida Ltd. Used by permission of Oneida Ltd. Silversmiths, Oneida, N.Y. The Philadelphia Inquirer, Today Magazine supplement: Two covers from the Picture Parade: "Wearing of the Green," March 17, 1940, and "Spirit of '76," June 30, 1940. Used by permission. The Prudential Insurance Company of America: "The Prudential Girl—1916," painted by W. Haskell Coffin. Copyright 1916. Reprinted by permission of The Prudential Insurance Company of America. R. J. Reynolds Industries, Inc.: Two advertisements for Camels Cigarettes: "Of Course Women Prefer Them," copyright 1931, R. J. Reynolds Tobacco Co., and "Same Girl...Same Smile...Same Cigarette." By permission of R. J. Reynolds Tobacco Company. Rheingold Breweries Inc.: Advertisement for Rheingold. Copyright 1949 by Liebmann Breweries, Inc., New York, N. Y. Used by permission. Jos. Schlitz Brewing Company: Advertisement for Schlitz. Copyright 1943, Jos. Schlitz Brewing Co. Used by permission. Shapiro, Bernstein & Co. Inc., 10 East 53rd St., New York, N.Y. 10022: "What a Wonderful Mother You'd Be," sheet-music cover. Copyright MCMXV by Shapiro, Bernstein & Co. Inc. Renewed. "Your Wife," sheet-music cover and lyrics. Copyright MCMXVI by Shapiro, Bernstein & Co. Inc. Renewed. Shawnee Press, Inc.: "Woman Forever March," sheet-music cover. Copyright © MCMXVI, E. T. Paull. U.S. Copyright Renewed. Copyright assigned to Shawnee Press, Inc., Delaware Water Gap, Pa. 18327. Used with permission. Skinner And Kennedy Co.: "The Little Princess," paper fan. Painted by M. R. Harris. Copyright by Arthur Francis Scheer. Copyright renewed. Harry Tobias, song lyricist: "Girl of My Dreams." Copyright 1920. Renewed by Harry Tobias. Alberto Vargas: "Do the New York; Ziegfeld Follies, 1931" sheet-music cover. Painting by Alberto Vargas. Copyright 1931 by Miller Music Inc. White-Westinghouse Corporation: Advertisement for Westinghouse. Copyright © 1924, W.E. & M. Co. Used with permission.

PERSONAL ACKNOWLEDGMENTS

To George Heckroth of Royal Oak, Michigan, known to very few, whose own passion for paper collecting inspired me, who early on encouraged my interest, I owe a special debt of gratitude. I spent many evenings in his small, cluttered farmhouse, poring over the wonderful items he had collected in his seventy years and listening to his stories. Always, I would return home with some new treasure for my own collection.

The people who deal in paper are quite extraordinary. Operating from their homes in small towns or from cramped quarters in large cities, they have in common that will to unearth and to preserve small bits of American history. Their love and special intuition lead them to explore attics or long-deserted places in the hope of finding specimens that will please the collector. Three of these dealers to whom I am most indebted are Doris Huckle of East Jordan, Michigan; Gwen Goldman of Lafayette Hill, Pennsylvania; and Rose Smolin of Manhattan.

I also wish to thank some others who have graciously contributed items for this book: Geno Sartori of "Brandon Memorabilia," Sandra Elm and Jack Banning of "Yesterday," and "The Owl Shoppe," all of Manhattan, and Joan Meyerowitz of Milford, Connecticut. Also, friends Bruce Nelson, Gene Szafran, and Drew Eliot, who have loaned items from their collections for use in this book.

Thanks also to Downe Publishing Company, publishers of Ladies' Home Journal, and to Time, Incorporated; and very special thanks to my publisher, Pantheon Books, who did so much to lighten my work, and to Virginia Barber, who encouraged me.

My most emphatic gratitude is given to Paul Gamarello, the designer, who by his own standard of excellence added brilliantly to the achievement of this book.

Contents

NOTES ON PICTURES

Postcards, trading cards, baseball, war, and bubble-gum cards dominated my childhood in Detroit in the 1940s. I collected these, as did practically every schoolchild, hoarded them in shoeboxes, and sorted them according to favorites. Also, I collected postage stamps, match covers, and movie pin-ups. Life was made richer by a plethora of printed paper, much the same as it is today by television, Kodachrome prints, and art reproductions.

My classroom walls were a showcase of heroic fantasy. It was wartime. There were posters for bond drives and the Red Cross, and there were glorious full-color portraits of all the presidents. Walls were decorated with prints of the flag and the Statue of Liberty. Great presidents and waving flags made me feel proud to be an American.

Pictures delighted me. I remember licking remnants of vanilla ice cream from Dixie Cup lids in order to discover a new MGM star for my collection, which already numbered in the hundreds. I remember Sunday comic supplements: The Little King, Henry, Little Lulu. Picture stories that I understood. I remember gathering magazines from the neighbors and rushing home to tear out all of the thrilling reproductions of great paintings, as well as the Mobilgas advertisements that showed horses, and the Norman Rockwell covers.

I am not alone. Since mass-produced pictures first became available, people have collected them. Before that time, art works were the luxury of a privileged few who could either visit museums or afford to buy paintings.

This book consists entirely of art that was published between 1865 and 1945, the years during which printing was the primary source for mass communication in America. With the advent of steam-powered presses in 1865, tradesmen began to print small, sedate cards that could be given to customers. In the 1870s these cards appeared frequently, now illustrated with a variety of subjects, and by the 1880s the production of lavish, full-color advertising cards had become a major industry. Before the turn of the century, a shift was made from card to magazine advertisements in the efforts of businessmen to reach wider and wider audiences. During the next four decades, the artist-illustrator was much in demand, until inevitably the faster and less expensive medium of photography began to take over. In 1945, at the end of World War II, the need for popular illustrators had subsided, as the advertising industry turned to the use of radio and television and, more and more, magazines lost their popularity.

The first artists remained anonymous. Trained as craftsmen, many were limited to merely making copies of popular subjects. Only a handful of the artists developed a personal style or "made a name" for themselves. Those who did are largely missing from this book. People like Charles Dana Gibson and Edward Penfield are entirely missing. Norman Rockwell, James Montgomery Flagg, Alberto Vargas, and J.C. Leyendecker are represented here by one or two of their early works. On the other hand, there is a much greater representation of work by Howard Chandler Christy and Harrison Fisher, if only because they conformed so willingly to the popular-stereotype imagery with which this book deals. But the fact remains that the creators of over ninety percent of the pictures that appeared will remain unknown.

Their work was impersonal to a degree, reflecting ideals of beauty, health, and romance to a population that was suffering from overwork, sickness, and isolation. The artists were probably all male, and delighted in depicting the women of their dreams. In pursuit of perfection photos were retouched, all blemishes removed. Imagination was lifted to new heights by the male artist's concept of women; he created a profusion of utopian angels, rose-strewn maidens, and exotic temptresses. Apparently, people appreciated the simple subjects and the naive sentiments of artists who captured moments in a more perfect world where mothers gazed lovingly at children, where healthy girls romped in flowery meadows, and where household drudgery vanished. In a world where so much was wrong, the artist possessed the magic that made things right, and to the degree that pictures seem real, people were inclined to accept what the artist saw, in good faith. Magazines reached women everywhere, bringing them in touch with others who had similar frustrations and similar dreams, and with advertisers who spoke to their needs.

The pictures in this book are drawn from my collection of approximately 10,000 paper items, sometimes called Paper Americana. What is important about those which are included is that they are not unique, each subject having been reproduced by the thousands, perpetuating and satisfying some common need. What saves them from being boring or remote to us today is probably their tenderness or sentiment, though as works of art they are sometimes grossly exaggerated, ineptly drawn, and overzealous to reach the heart. These images have been taken from calendars and advertising cards; from paper keepsakes such as fans, paper dolls, and booklets; from <u>cartes de visite</u>, stereopticon views, and cabinet photos, which were largely made prior to 1900; and from prints, postcards, sheet-music covers, magazine covers, and magazine advertisements, which were used more prolifically after 1900. They were almost always produced in rich, full color, the earlier pieces by color lithography, and later ones by myriads of innovations in the printing industry. In order to focus upon the theme of the portrayal of women, I have sometimes disassociated the pictures from their intended use as music covers, posters, and so on. I have chosen to concentrate on related thematic material rather than chronology.

Through such arrangement, the myth becomes apparent, just as through the process of collecting, the idea for this book become apparent. Myths prevail. Here, all the expected roles of women are illustrated, from romantic elopement, blushing bride, and honeymoon to household drudge and nagging wife. The same myths are repeated in song lyrics which date from the same period. All are expressions of feeling made viable through art.

Mickey Mouse looms large in the hearts of Americans, as does Uncle Sam. Aunt Jemima and the Campbell's Soup Kids are known to all. We tend to sympathize with the mythological creations of artists. The real people who graced the pages of the same magazines were less endearing. The Amelia Earharts and Jane Addamses do not hold such a cherished spot. We are more inclined to pattern our lives after Hollywood stars and astrological stars, comic books and love stories. We are inclined to dream. And yes, to seek after the popular and most common objects of a generation past, to value the treasures of flea market and memorabilia shop in much the same way another culture might collect its old masters. Of this I too am guilty. We place high value on the scrapbooks, photo albums, and magazines first hoarded and then discarded by our grandparents. Now as always, impassioned picture collectors will be found in unrelenting pursuit, re-collecting the collections put lovingly together by someone, stored in old shoeboxes, and sorted according to favorites. Perhaps today's myth will be tomorrow's nostalgia.

CAROL WALD

INTRODUCTION

In past centuries it was assumed that God had determined man's and woman's roles in life and had formed them accordingly, providing each with a body and a temperament appropriate to their different functions. The man, as husband, provider, and head of the family, was distinct from the woman, who was wife, mother, and keeper of the house. Today these assumptions have been challenged, and a great debate has developed concerning the nature of woman—and consequently, of man as well. The controversy rages: What is the real nature of the female human? How much does biology determine sex roles and personality? Is there such a thing as a "natural" woman? How much does the society in which people develop influence the formation of "male" and "female" characteristics?

In view of the controversy, this collection of popular images of women from America's past is especially timely and provocative. Many of the pictures have a nostalgic charm and are amusing to look at from the perspective of the 1970s. But <u>Myth America</u> also provides food for thought. What are these pictures? Cards, calendars, sheet-music covers, advertisements, prints, and postcards, all of which portray women at work and at play, growing up, looking beautiful, being naughty, being good, courting, marrying, keeping house, and raising children. The pictures were part of the ordinary life of their time, commonly found in people's houses, in shops, and in places of business. What did they mean to people in the past? What do these popular images tell us today in 1975?

The period they describe, between the last third of the nineteenth century and the middle of the twentieth, was one of the most dramatic in American history. During these eighty years, sweeping changes took place that affected almost everyone. In 1865, Americans generally lived on farms and in small rural towns. Most of them, or their ancestors, had emigrated from the British Isles. White and Protestant, they lived in a world seldom influenced by the Indians, who had been pushed aside, and the Afro-Americans, mostly contained in the Southern states. In the international world, the United States was a small although growing power, and its role in world affairs was minor.

Even before the Civil War, which began in 1861, important aspects of American life had begun to change; by the 1880s, these changes were proceeding with dizzying speed, affecting men and women alike throughout the land.

Industrialization, large-scale immigration from Europe and Asia, and a vast migration of Americans from the country to the city destroyed old patterns of life and forced new styles of living to develop rapidly. As the years passed, increasing numbers of Americans earned their livings not on the farm but in factories and cities. Millions of immigrants, along with discontented and impoverished farmers and farm laborers, filled the cities to bursting and turned small towns into metropolises almost overnight. As the decades of the 1900s rolled along, the changes continued. Soon, most Americans lived in cities and their suburbs. (Today, over two-thirds of us do.) We had become one of the most industrialized societies in the world; we were rich and powerful, and increasingly involved in world affairs.

Such dramatic changes touched almost everyone. In a relatively short span of years, between one generation and the next, the nature of daily life, within the family and within the larger community, altered radically. People worked at new and strange jobs, unlike those of their parents or grandparents; they lived in different kinds of dwellings, in tenements and apartment houses, and in cities without grass; they sought relaxation in new ways. The population of the United States had become a mosaic of many religious, racial, and ethnic parts, a complex and heterogeneous mass in which men and women had to find new places and new relationships for themselves. Beneath the changing exterior of life, the very structure of personal experience was changing.

Every human society has laws and customs that serve to give it structure and order, guiding and limiting human behavior according to defined and accepted standards. In some societies, the restrictions on behavior may be oppressive and onerous; in others, they may be loose and barely noticeable. But every ordered society has rules, and authorities that make and enforce them. In the United States, in the era before the Civil War, these authorities were the church, the family, and the local community; they defined and enforced the patterns of acceptable behavior. Parents and grandparents served as models for children, making clear what young people were to be like as they matured: men lived and worked as their fathers had; women, as their mothers. The church offered regular instruction, family and church preached the same rules, and the small community in which people grew up and usually remained monitored the lives of its members. By the time a person reached adulthood, there was little question or doubt about what he or she was to do and be like and little opportunity to deviate without difficulty.

Imagine the change when men and women moved from small towns and farm communities to vast metropolitan areas. Small apartments and houses split the large family and separated generations from each other. People worked at jobs that were completely different from their fathers' and their mothers'. Home and work were in two different locations, sometimes far away from each other. Daily, people rushed from one part of the city to another by trolleys, subways, and automobiles. This new style of life brought with it a strange new personal privacy that had not been possible in small rural communities. Men and women carried on their daily business insulated and isolated from each other in the impersonal city. Parents, church, and community grew apart and became increasingly less influential in transmitting models and monitoring behavior.

New rule makers appeared in their stead. Schools became more important in children's lives, substituting for much of what parents and churches had done before. Governments, too, played a growing role in the individual's life, offering services that churches and church charities had performed and expecting in return certain kinds of behavior, as the churches had.

Business and industry also assumed importance and authority. New industries, for example, were the major agents in transforming both the European peasant and the American-born farmer into an efficient factory worker, breaking men and women of rural habits and attitudes and habituating them (often with difficulty) to the time clock, the assembly line, and new concepts of work and wealth.

Moreover, in developing and advertising manufactured products, American industries affected the lives of the entire population. People who had recently produced most of their own clothing and foodstuffs and who had inherited rich craft traditions and skills soon became large-scale consumers of manufactured goods and processed foods, willing purchasers of the vast array of products turned out by the industrial plants of the nation.

Methods of large-scale communication became an important and interesting aspect of this changing society. Before the Civil War, there were relatively few means of mass communication, and those were slow and costly. But in the industrial era, lithographic printing and photoduplication grew less expensive and more widespread, as did education. As a result, magazines, newspapers, and books became regular facts of everyday life during the second half of the nineteenth century. Printed words and images entered into the experience of ordinary people and became an important means by which rules and standards were defined and disseminated (as radio and television were to function later in the twentieth century). By the end of the 1800s, the profusion of printed words and images often served as parents and grandparents had, bombarding young children with models of acceptable behavior and with social and cultural values, shaping the forms of perception and thought. It is these images that are printed in the following chapters.

The new imagery was particularly important for women. Representations of women dominated the abundant printing, advertising products, decorating calendars, and gracing postcards. Like flowers, birds, cherubs, and flaming sunsets, female faces and figures were commonly used by artists and photographers. As decorative elements, they were attached to products as diverse as jewelry, tobacco, soap powder, sailboats, and books, used to catch attention, please, and sell. Beyond decoration, images of women also became symbols. The young girl, the mother with babe, and the kindly grandmother represented the American way of life, its family relationships, economic structure, and religious ethic. In war as well as in peace, Miss America symbolized the nation.

In addition, the bulk of mass-media advertising was directed at women who as housewives were the major consumers in the country, general purchasing agents for the family. As the range and quantity of manufactured goods increased in the twentieth century, more and more advertisements told women what to buy in order to care for their families properly. But they did much more than this because, invariably, the ads conveyed complex messages. At the same time that they urged women to buy a particular product, they also implied that using that product would make the buyer the kind of woman she was supposed to be. Consider, for example, an advertisement for shortening: this brand of shortening, the message says, enables every girl to make the perfect pie; the perfect girl, the message implies, wants to make the perfect pie; indeed, one who makes a perfect pie is a perfect girl. In noncommercial prints as well as ads, most of the women portrayed are young, pretty, and feminine. Repeated tens of thousands of times, these images said, in effect, that women should be young, feminine, and attractive.

Thus popular imagery functions in a complex way. It reflects popular views since it aims to please and persuade the viewer, but it also influences popular attitudes since the repeated messages form and reinforce standards and norms. The prints and photos in Myth America mirror changes that took place in women's lives after the Civil War; while the images themselves functioned as agents of change, introducing new standards of behavior and encouraging conformity to them. Changing clothing styles, for example, are readily apparent. Around the middle of the 1800s, women were well covered; long skirts, long sleeves, and thick corsets disguised and hid their bodies. As the decades pass, they are slowly but surely uncovered. By the twentieth century, female bodies are out of hiding and revealed to be beautiful and, increasingly, sexual. The activities in which women participate also change. Nineteenth-century women were domestic and retiring. By the turn of the century, women are shown on the golf course and in factories. Modern women are more active and involved in the world outside the house than their predecessors. Their manner is very different. The older images portray childlike, angelic, and rather sexless women. As time marches on, the images become flirtatious and sexual. And sometimes, they show women in studious roles, beneath mortarboards in academic robes, as attitudes toward higher education for women changed.

While many things can be seen to change, much remains the same. According to these prints and photographs, certain attributes and characteristics of women are constant. In the 1940s as in the 1880s, the American woman is maternal and gentle. She stays sweet and pretty. Even as she moves into the factory or the shop, even as she swings her tennis racket or mounts her bicycle, she remains, in these pages, a feminine creature.

The images that follow are mythical images—idealizations and abstractions of women who never existed. At the same time they are very real, since they were powerful and important forces guiding and molding the attitudes of women and men in the course of our history.

Reality consists of substituting a new set of myths for the old.

—Milton Covensky, Detroit, Michigan, 1975

SUGAR & SPICE

Everything Nice

Training-up Little Girls

"Higher Education"

**Sugar and spice, and everything nice;
That's what little girls are made of.**

— Nursery rhyme

Dominant among the many images of women that are portrayed in <u>Myth America</u> are those of childlike creatures—sweet, simple, virtuous, wide-eyed. Looking carefully at the little girls pictured in this chapter, one discovers characteristics that are repeated over and over in the portrayal of adult women. Whether they are sweethearts, mothers, angels, housecleaners, college students, or secretaries, they continue to resemble these little girls; they are consistently sweet, innocent and unknowing, always pretty and rather fluffy. As they grow older, they retain their childish nature. Their innocence and simplicity seem permanent; age and experience never transform these attributes into wisdom or sophistication.

In past centuries, children were treated as little adults, small versions of grownups. (The special status that they have today, with its privileges and indulgences, is a recent phenomenon, a side effect of contemporary life, affluence, and psychology.) These little girls are nineteenth-century products: they are literally "little women." As soon as they can move about, they reveal their feminine nature. They play at being mothers and housekeepers. Again and again, advertisements show children performing women's work—cleaning, mending, caring for babies. Such pictures tell the viewer several things: a particular soap makes scrubbing clothes so simple even a girl-child can do the laundry; moreover, one who uses the soap will be young and fresh; scrubbing clothes is female work.

It is interesting to see that the image of the American woman does not change very much even when she goes to college. Higher learning does not take the stars out of her eyes. Playful and pretty as ever, a decoration and mascot, she remains the child-woman, innocent and unknowing.

What was the reality behind these images?

Surely not all little girls were pretty or sweet, or as clean and compliant as these cherubs. Some certainly preferred riding horses or climbing trees to washing and sweeping. Farm children, male and female, were agricultural workers, and poor city girls went into factories and sweatshops before they reached puberty. What kind of women did _they_ grow up to be? Where, in these pictures of childlike women, are the hardworking, careworn, and mature women of the past?

In 1850, higher education for women seemed unnecessary and even harmful to many people. Fifty years later, however, educational opportunities for women were increasing, especially for those from prosperous families, as women's colleges and state universities offered a small, fortunate group what had always been considered a man's education.

Nonetheless, in the popular portrayal of women, behind the sweet and simple face of the childlike female still lurked the suggestion of an inferior intelligence. It was an old idea: women were thought to have smaller and different brains from men. The idea persists in the girl-woman pictured in these pages, and although it conflicted with the reality of the woman who was taking her place as a mature and productive person in American life, it remained to shadow her entrance into the twentieth century.

SUGAR & SPICE
EVERYTHING NICE

A creature not too bright or good
For human nature's daily food;
For transient sorrows, simple wiles,
Praise, blame, love, kisses, tears, and smiles.

—William Wordsworth (quoted in Singer Sewing Machine advertisement, 1901)

NOBODY LOVES ME.

ATER'S PILLS.

GOOD NIGH

Have you a little FAIRY in your home?

14

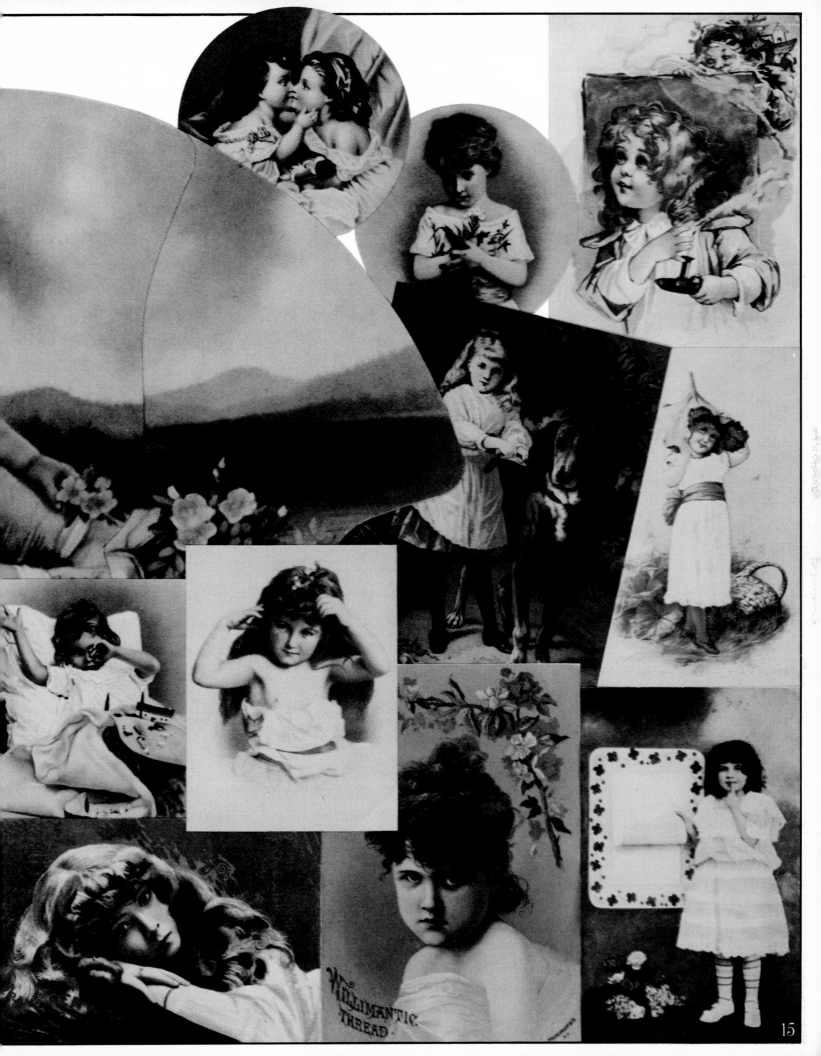

15

SUGAR ◈ SPICE
TRAINING-UP LITTLE GIRLS

COPYRIGHTED, 1892.   MY BUSY DAY.   over

It is for the parents to educate their daughters for the profession of housewives. To become an efficient housewife, it needs the early training that a man has to undergo to become a mechanic, a professional man, or a trader. Men will more respect a girl who can use a little French "bons-mots" in the parlor. Her white and flexible hands will lose none of their charms if they are pricked by the industrious needle. The wife thus employed will have more respect for herself, and will be a good judge of the hardships of her husband. The husband will love the little sprite who lessens his anxieties and affords him so much comfort.

—William H. Walling, A.M., M.D., Sexology, Philadelphia, 1904

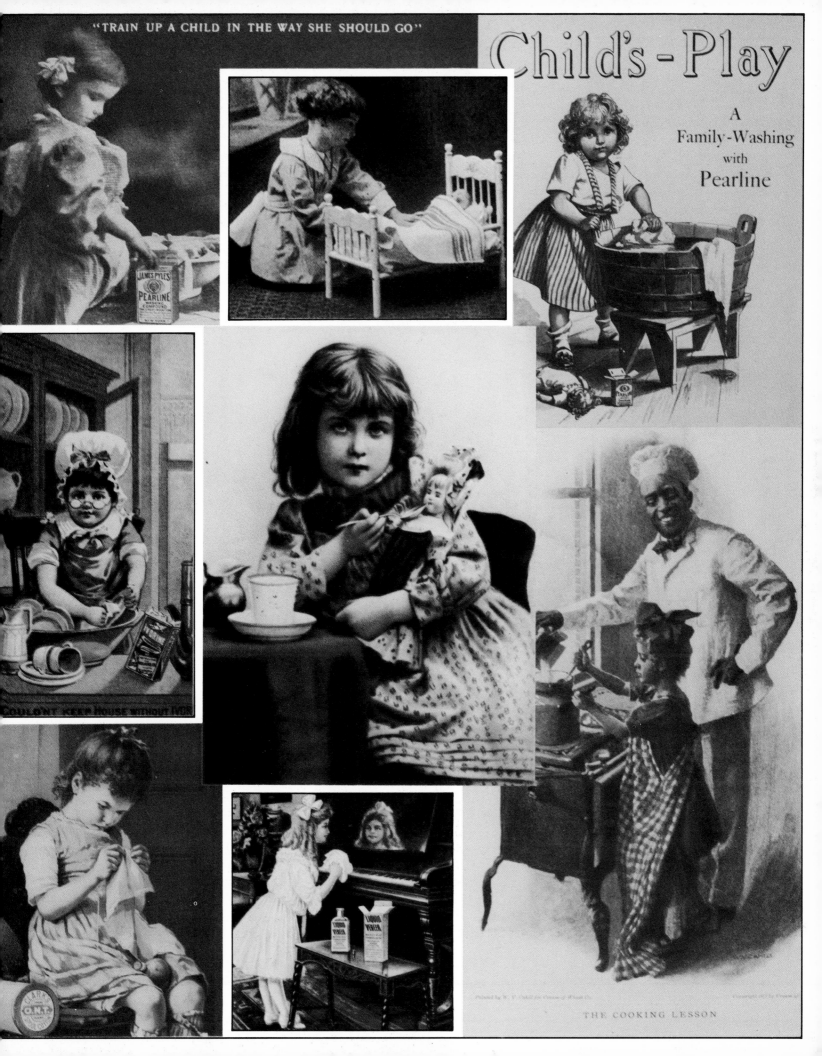

Every young girl's ambition
—to make a perfect pie

Stirring the JELL-O into a pint of boiling water. It dissolves immediately.

The simple process of making and serving is illustrated in this series of four pictures.

How's That, Grandma?

Helping Mother

Bake at Ho

USE YEAST

AND SAVE MONEY

MAZOLA

RYZON

The college maiden,
Her head is laden,
With a knowledge not
Consisting all of Greek;

She sings a solo,
Plays well at polo,
For football and fencing
Honors now she seeks;

She is a stunner,
She is a runner,
And excels in ev'ry sport,
She takes a whirl;

Also a beauty
In classroom duty,
Is the flashing, dashing,
Modern College Girl.

—Song Lyric, "The College Girl," 1903

HIGHER EDUCATION

Winning Faces

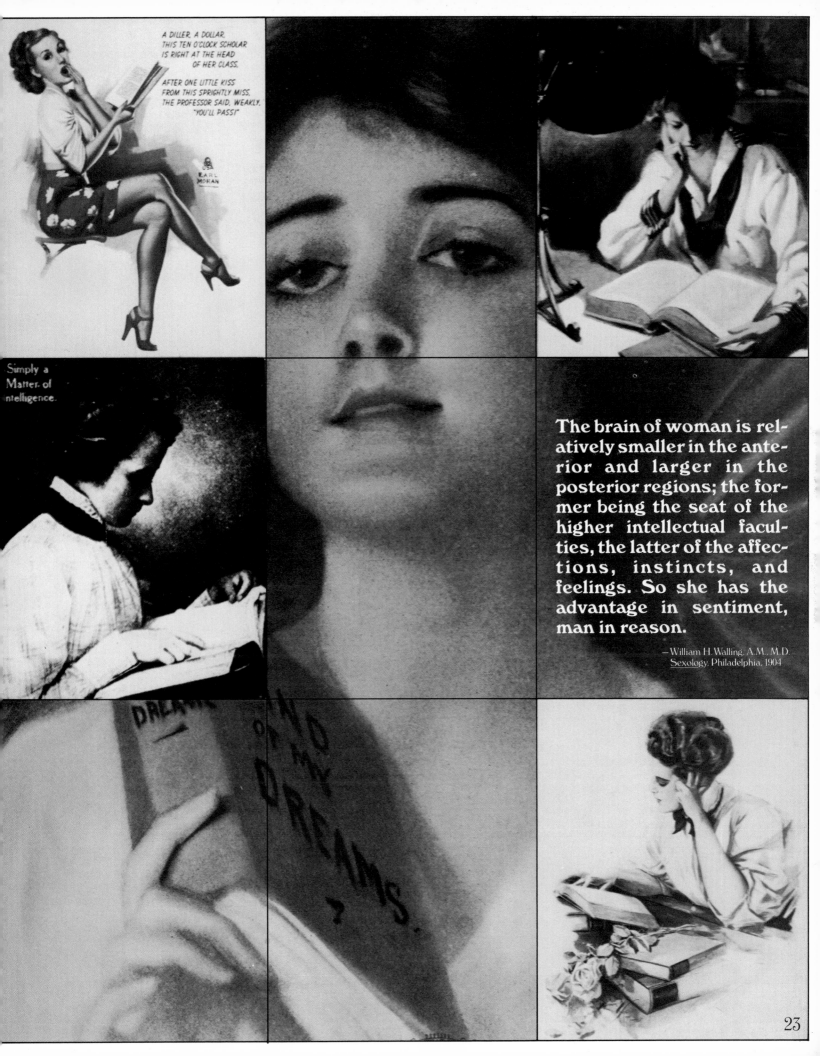

A DILLER, A DOLLAR,
THIS TEN O'CLOCK SCHOLAR
IS RIGHT AT THE HEAD
OF HER CLASS.

AFTER ONE LITTLE KISS
FROM THIS SPRIGHTLY MISS,
THE PROFESSOR SAID, WEAKLY,
"YOU'LL PASS!"

EARL
MORAN

Simply a
Matter. of
intelligence.

The brain of woman is relatively smaller in the anterior and larger in the posterior regions; the former being the seat of the higher intellectual faculties, the latter of the affections, instincts, and feelings. So she has the advantage in sentiment, man in reason.

—William H. Walling. A.M., M.D.
Sexology. Philadelphia, 1904

The College Girl

NO INTELLIGENCE REQUIRED

—in the Use of PEARLINE—but in the selection of it—YES! Simply SOAK or BOIL and RINSE—and the Washing is done—that's SIMPLE enough for a child. BUT—to desert the thousand year's old bar-soap-way and to realize that PEARLINE IS MODERN SOAP and to look back on it's thirty years of general use—it's Millions of Users and Friends and Absence of Enemies—there's where Intelligence gets the better of the Dull Ones and accepts the Benefits of PEARLINE.

No woman objects to being called intelligent provided she is assured that it has done no harm to her looks.

—Aubrey Menen (1912-   )

GOOD/BAD GIRLS GIRLS

| Pious and Pure |
| Naughty and Nice |

> **When she was good she was very, very good,**
> **But when she was bad she was horrid.**
>
> —Henry Wadsworth Longfellow, 1882

The idea that girls (and women) are horrid if they are not very, very good is an old and recurrent theme in Western cultures, reaching back beyond the nursery rhyme. The founders of the Christian church authoritatively decreed that women were either virgins or whores: they either had no sexuality, a characteristic of virgins and angels, or some, which was too much! In more recent times, the Victorian fathers embraced this idea fervently, and invigorated it. These nineteenth-century moralists could comprehend only two kinds of females. Good women were interested in religion, uninterested in sex, and innately inclined to take care of things — families and houses. Bad women, depraved, inferior creatures, not only had sexual feelings but found them gratifying. In between good and bad, there was an abyss. One step down from the Victorian pedestal and a woman fell all the way.

This view was popular, especially among middle-class Americans, about the time of the Civil War. A good woman stayed happily at home, where her talents and inclinations were fulfilled, or she went to church. Angels, as we know, are not very assertive. Their pictures clearly show that they are unlikely to resist or dispute; devils, not angels, make trouble. The concept of the fallen woman was equally felicitous. Confirming the fragility of female virtue, it provided fit partners for the sexual activities of Victorian men, who turned out to be, good and bad alike, very sexual creatures.

By the end of the 1800s, during America's tumultuous passage from rural agricultural life to urban industrialized society, almost everyone's way of life was changing, including that of the domesticated virgin of Victorianism. She remained, of course, a wife, mother, and homemaker, still more virtuous than most men. But somewhere between the pedestal and the brothel, a new place was developing for her.

In most human experience, sex has been coupled with fertility and childbearing; Western religions have preached that the only purpose of and justification for sex was reproduction. But by the end of the nineteenth century, troublesome questions were arising as a result of the increasing acceptance and practice of birth control. If sex was not to be rationalized as the means of making babies, what was it all about? What was to come of the good women whose sex lives had been seen as auxiliary to childbearing? Were they to be transformed suddenly into sexual creatures?

At the time these questions were being raised, the function of the middle-class woman in the home was changing. Small families, cheap servants, and modern technology were lightening and eliminating some of her traditional tasks. What would be her role in the twentieth century?

One alternative led toward activities outside the home in the public world, in employment, the arts, or politics. Another direction was offered within the private sphere by the "naughty and nice" image that is illustrated in these pages, where the Victorian angel is replaced by a new sexual woman. Actually, the concept of the sexless woman had been a controversial "fact" and an uneasy social reality among Victorians themselves. By the end of the 1800s, psychologists and intellectuals as well as advertisers had joined the dissenters to propose that women were naturally endowed with sexual needs and feelings.

Thus between the pedestal and the brothel emerged a sexual role for wives and sweethearts. If they dressed properly, used cosmetics carefully, strove for a delicate balance between virgin and whore, a whole new aspect of life was available to good women. "Naughty and nice" was the debut of the sexual woman of the twentieth century.

GOOD GIRLS / BAD GIRLS

PIOUS & PURE

Are you from Heaven?
My glad heart sings.
Are you an angel?
Where are your wings?
Who were you sent for?
Who were you meant for?
I'll tell you, I'll tell you,
For me alone!

Your smile is sunshine,
Your tears are dew,
Your eyes are starlight,
So pure and true.
Your Godly splendor,
Your soul so tender,
Are you from Heaven?
Please tell me, do.

—Song lyric, "Are You from Heaven?", 1917

Best Christmas Greetings

Women are the poetry of the world in the same sense as the stars are the poetry of heaven.— Clear, light-giving, harmonious, they are the terrestrial planets that rule the destinies of mankind.

— Francis Hargrave (1741-1821)

The First Composite Madonna in the World

How the Kitchell Composite Madonna of 271 Paintings of the Virgin Mother was Made

TO NO other woman has the world ever given so much of its love and reverence as to the Virgin Mother of Christ. For ages she has been the highest and holiest type of motherhood known to mankind, and age after age the greatest painters of all time have striven to realize humanity's ideal of her, until the number of Madonnas is greater than that of any other single class of pictures in existence. To sum up the combined loveliness and spiritual charm of the most representative and beautiful of these master paintings in one transcendent face was the idea which first occurred to Joseph Gray Kitchell, the originator of this unique type of Madonna, as he was riding from Denver to Boulder in Colorado, skirting the foothills of the Rocky Mountains, late one brilliant afternoon toward the end of September, 1889.

The Madonna in art was already a subject of interest to him. So it was not far from mind that afternoon when the recollection of some recent observations happened to lead to the casual reflection that Americans are composites of many national types. Possibly the glowing Colorado sunset, with its wealth of color and later fading aureole, yellow as gold-dust, above the distant peaks, helped to recall at just the right moment the rich tints and bright halo of Madonna art. Be that as it may, the thought of the blending of numerous nationalities suddenly connected itself with the remembrance of the many paintings of the Madonna, and the idea of making an effort to merge them into one supreme type took form. Photography, it was evident, was the only means by which such a result could be attained, and the preliminary task of collecting the necessary material was soon after begun.

SOME of the photographs of the original pictures were bought; others were taken, where the privilege could be secured; and during the next seven or eight years, in which two trips abroad were made and many European galleries and art centres visited, several hundred prints were brought together. Most of these were of varying sizes, however, and the first need was to enlarge the smaller ones and reduce the bigger ones so as to bring all to one uniform scale.

THIS work was combined with that of the actual production of the composite picture, and was carried to completion during spare hours, first in Madison, Wisconsin, and then in Indianapolis, Indiana, in the course of about two years and a half. Methods and apparatus for overcoming difficulties and simplifying the task had been previously thought out or invented. Paintings of a generally similar character were grouped together; a composite picture of each group was made; and these group composites were finally merged into the present picture. Perfected lenses of Jena glass and special photographic plates were used, and an ingeniously simple contrivance was devised for making sure, before a print was photographed, that its eye, nose and mouth lines coincided accurately with those already on the plate.

The use of this apparatus led to one curiously surprising discovery—that the faces of many of the Madonnas painted by the old masters were out of drawing, especially the eyes, one of which was not infrequently found to be higher or larger than the other. This mechanical defect appeared chiefly in the so-called portrait Madonnas, painted from living models, and was rarely to be detected in the paintings of a purely ideal type.

IN ALL two hundred and seventy-one Madonnas were combined in this one extraordinary face. The first intention was to include only old masterpieces, but later it was decided to make the result more completely representative by reproducing a sufficient number of the comparatively few famous Madonnas of recent times to maintain the proportion between them and the many great Madonnas of the Middle Ages. Nearly one-half the paintings included, therefore, belong to the sixteenth century, and about a third more to the fifteenth and seventeenth centuries, while the rest are almost evenly divided between the fourteenth and the eighteenth and nineteenth centuries. Of the great masters, Raphael, of course, is represented by the largest number of paintings, with Giovanni Bellini next, closely followed by Perugino, Andrea del Sarto, and Murillo, after whom come Guido Reni, Botticelli, Correggio, Titian, Rubens, Paul Veronese, Giotto, Filippo Lippi, Leonardo da Vinci, Albrecht Dürer, and Van Dyck. Of the moderns, Bouguereau is the best known.

FULL-FACE pictures were used almost exclusively, of course; but occasionally two three-quarter faces of similar aspect, turned in opposite directions, were combined, as in the case of Madonnas by Titian and Nicolas Poussin. Errors of line inseparable from the blending of so many faces naturally crept into the final picture, and needed to be corrected. This delicate task was intrusted to an American painter of Madonnas, Elliott Daingerfield, whose work consisted, to use his own words, in "a little surer placing of line and subtlety of modeling."

The result, which is now given on this page — of course, in smaller reproduction than in the prints in the art stores —has aroused strong interest among prominent people. Secretary Hay was "greatly struck by its beauty and finish"; Chief Justice Fuller found it "charming"; Henry Watterson wrote, "It is altogether the most perfect and beautiful conception which I have ever seen"; Booker T. Washington considered it a "beautiful work of art"; Joseph Jefferson had "never seen a Madonna with a more spiritual expression"; Madame Patti regarded it as "a most beautiful and original conception"; Sir Henry Irving found it "extremely interesting"; Edison thought it "very fine"; Marconi admired its "charm"; and Tesla declared it to be "inspired."

Other opinions, while questioning whether the face is beautiful, admit the power of its mystical appeal. To them its eyes are more than motherly, for they are the eyes of a virgin mother, and its tender sweetness and brooding calm are eloquent of the gentle quietude inseparable from the "Maid-Mother of the Lord of Life." In particular, they are filled with awe at finding that this Madonna of Madonnas bears a singular likeness to the face of the Christ as it is usually portrayed; and certainly it is a striking fact that the merging of all these ideals of the Madonna by the great painters of so many ages and lands into one face should result in the revelation of this strange resemblance between the Holy Mother and her Divine Son.

NO MATTER how opinions of the picture may differ, however, as they undoubtedly will, here is the unique result of the first attempt ever made to produce a composite Madonna by combining two hundred and seventy-one of the greatest Madonnas of the world.

O, what makes women lovely? Virtue, faith, and gentleness in suffering; an endurance through scorn or trial; these call beauty forth, give it the stamp celestial, and admit into sisterhood with angels.

— Sir Nathaniel Brent (1575–1652)

A Happy Christmas

33

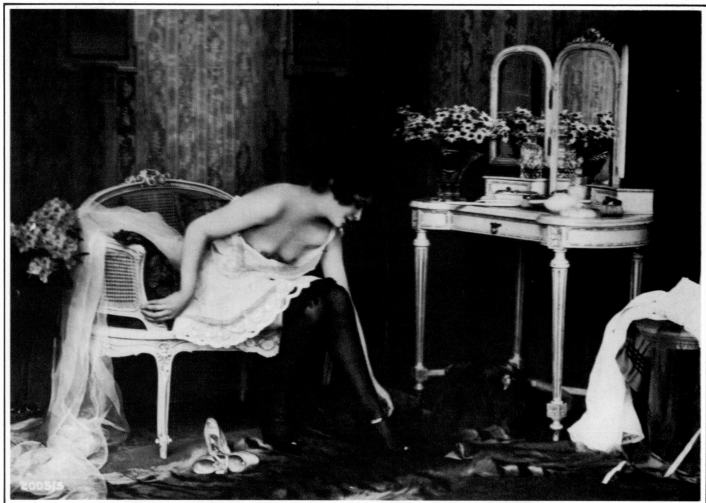

NAUGHTY & NICE

You are pettish and coquettish,
fickle, always in a whirl!
For your eyes so brightly flashing
show me you're that sort of girl.
—Song lyric, "The Dollar Princess," 1909

You'd say she was a portrait
of innocence and grace,
Be careful of
the innocence and grace!
Monday she was blushing
like a piece of peachy fruit,
Be careful of
the little peachy fruit!
On Thursday she had
nailed me in a breach of
promise suit,
Be careful of the
"breach of promise" suit.

—Song lyric. "The Harmless
Little Girl with the
Downcast Eyes," 1896

Call To-morrow

You can have my number

Some are so uncharitable as to think all women bad, and others are so credulous as to believe they are all good. All will grant her corporeal frame more wonderful and more beautiful than man's. And can we think God would put a worse soul into her better body?

—Owen Feltham (1602-1668)

Is This What You'd like to See?

To Reno for Mine

Out of Control

Compel me not to toe the mark,
Be ever prim and true;
But rather let me do those things
That I ought not to do.

—Postcard verse, 1910

39

ZIEGFELD FOLLIES
GLORIFYING THE AMERICAN GIRL
LYRICS AND MUSIC BY
J. P. MURRAY
BARRY TRIVERS
BEN OAKLAND
MACK GORDON
HARRY REVEL
GENE BUCK
DAVE STAMPER
AND OTHERS
PUBLISHED BY
MILLER MUSIC
INCORPORATED
62 WEST 45TH ST. N.Y.C.

"Gypsy Queen Cigarettes."

"Compliments of 'Old Judge.'"

His Affinity—

Give to me the Broadway Girl!
You may have your seashore pearl!
If she comes from Broadway,
She's the one for me, say—
You can bet she's in the whirl,
From her toes to topmost curl!
She's an all right New York Girl.
She's it, for my money!
She's the only oneie!
Give to me the Broadway Girl!

—Song lyric, "The Broadway Girl," 1904

HAYMARKET THEATRE BLDG.
161 West Madison Street
CHICAGO

A Good Pair to Draw to.

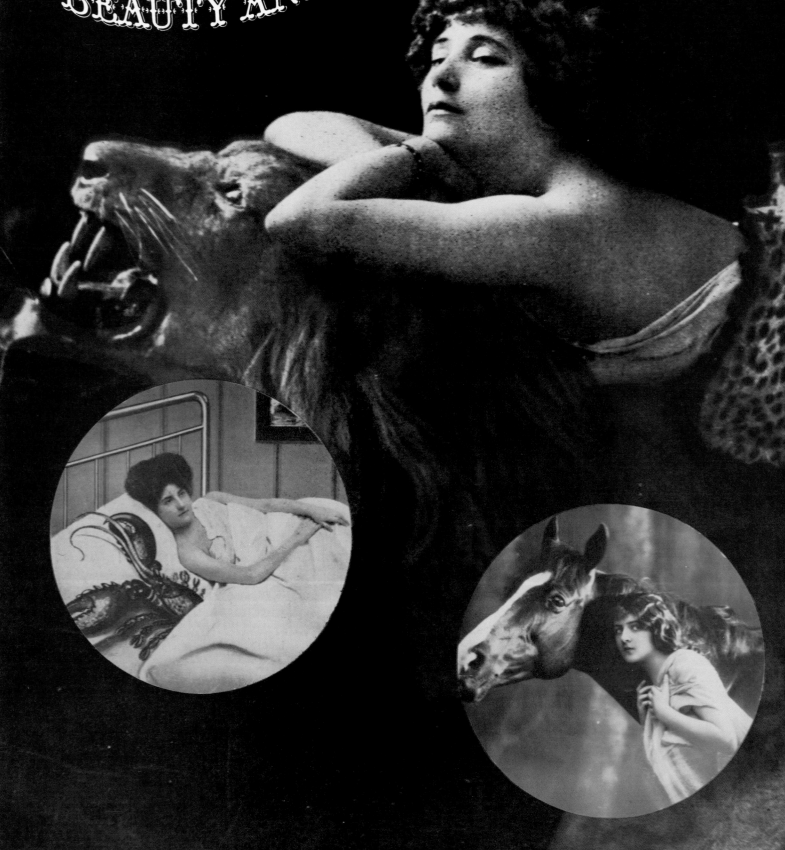

BEAUTY AND THE BEAST

FUN AND FROLIC

| The Outdoor Girl |
| Sports |
| Belles-Artes |

**Some think the world is made for fun and frolic,
And so do I, and so do I.**

—Song lyric, "Funiculi, Funicula," 1880

The men and women who founded this nation believed that work glorified God and idleness did not, and well into the nineteenth century, "fun and frolic" were considered wasteful, even sinful. Recreation as we know and enjoy it today was relatively rare.

Moreover, easy, informal contact between the sexes was also frowned upon, especially by citizens with social pretensions. Women's activities were confined to home and church. They were also limited by the common Victorian belief that ladies were physically delicate, and constrained by clothing that denied them freedom. Middle-class women regularly carried about fifteen pounds of skirts and crinolines, while steel-ribbed corsets pushed in mercilessly on their ribs, stomachs, and livers. They could not run, bend, walk, or breathe easily. The country was, of course, full of frontier women, poor working women, and until the Civil War, slave women who lifted and labored manfully. But the contrast did not stop affluent Americans from viewing their women as frail. In fact, the delicacy of one's wife was a sign of social and economic status: only a man of means could afford a physically weak and useless wife.

In the pages that follow, we can see a society in change, as the power of these Puritan and Victorian ideas fades. During the 1800s, recreation became more acceptable for both men and women. Living more and more in crowded cities, Americans discovered fresh air and wanted exercise. In the 1880s, bicycling was a national craze. Then golf and tennis became popular. In the twentieth century, sports and entertainment became a way of life; they were beautiful, healthy, and moral. And soon they were also commercialized. One needed not only to relax but to relax in the appropriate clothing and costumes and with the proper equipment in hand.

These changes were very important to women. Covered to the ankles, they began to play polite games of croquet and to participate in mixed bathing parties. Slowly women moved on to the tricycle and then the bicycle. By the 1900s, they played golf and tennis, softball and basketball. They also fished, camped, drove automobiles, and even flew airplanes.

Women's participation in recreation mirrored their progress from the confines of Victorianism to the larger world. As they became more active, their clothing of necessity changed to permit increasing freedom. The disappearance over the decades of corsets, crinolines, and skirts represented tangible gains in freedom.

Despite the liberation of their bodies, there are no powerful, muscular, or serious athletes here. Instead we see playful, coy, and sometimes inept women cavorting about. The bathing beauty splashes in the surf and suns on the sand, but hardly ever swims. Sports are fun and frolic, not athletics. Moreover, these playful women often are part of a sentimental view of nature—a potpourri of flowers, birds, waterfalls, children, and nymphs—that appeals to Americans increasingly cooped up in cities and cut off from outdoor life.

These portrayals of American women at play, with expensive equipment in hand, seem to have little in common with the lives of poor people who struggled daily with the burdens of rapid industrialization and agricultural depression. Cities teemed with immigrants and migrants, and millions of women, and men, toiled in factories and sweatshops with hardly an opportunity for fun and frolic. And yet, in a strange way, the women in these pictures had a real place in everyone's lives because they symbolized leisure and success, lighthearted sport, and wholesome good times; they were beguiling images of the good life.

FUN
AND FROLIC
THE OUTDOOR GIRL

**We love the Yachting-girl in white,
She looks so sweet and pure and bright.**

—Postcard verse, 1906

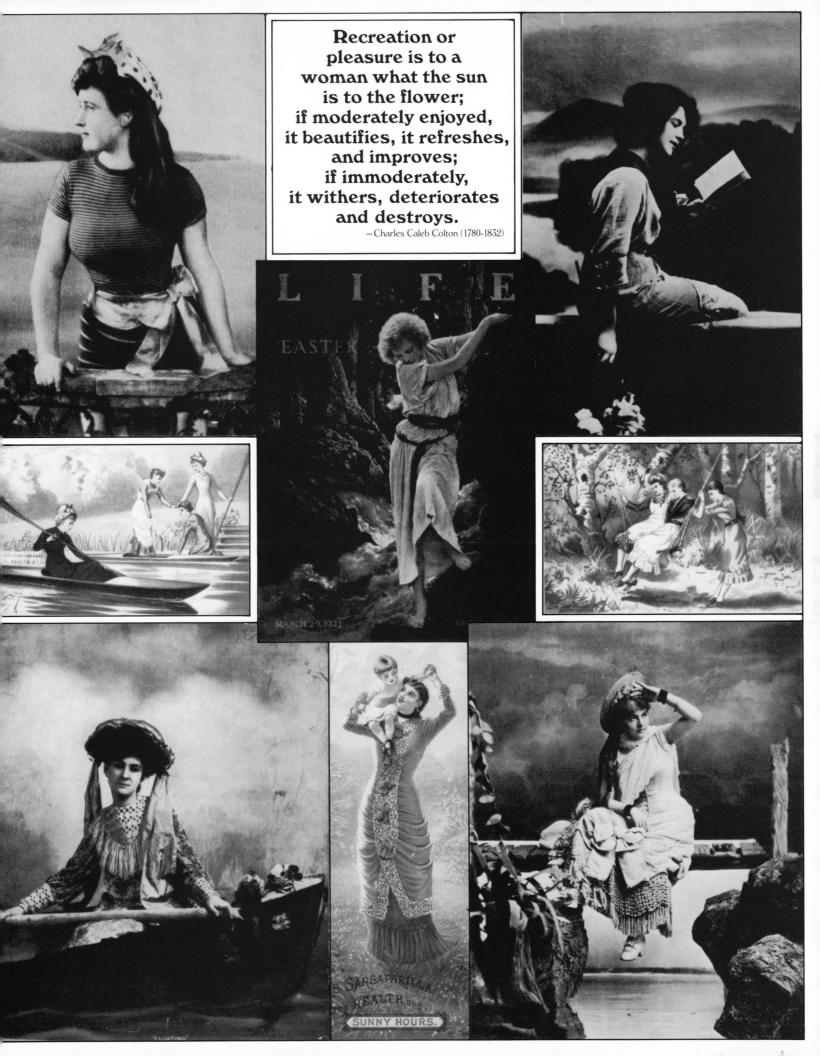

Recreation or
pleasure is to a
woman what the sun
is to the flower;
if moderately enjoyed,
it beautifies, it refreshes,
and improves;
if immoderately,
it withers, deteriorates
and destroys.

—Charles Caleb Colton (1780-1832)

Play Ball

A maid took a notion
To see why the ocean
    Had such a clear indigo hue
So she gave all the slip
Went in for a dip
    And found it was
Wiggle=Stick BLUE

Seaside, Oregon."

KEANSBURG

88 All alone.

All Wool and a Yard Wide.
Asbury Park, N. J.

HAPPY AS CAN BE.

Here's looking at you.

AYER'S HAIR V...

A. H. V. FOR THE TOILET

54

FUN
AND FROLIC

Sports

Women do not aim for an athlete's prodigious strength, but for
the development of each muscle of the body to uniform strength
and symmetry, giving those curves and lines of beauty which have
made the feminine figure the model for all sculptors and painters.

—Advertisement, Physical Culture
Extension Work in America, 1904

Serves you right

The Girl of the Y.W.
...elp us put ...he
...iangle
top!

BELLES OF THE BALL
Basket Ball Team, Normal School, No. 2, Wash...

Your tennis champion by day will be adorable tonight in a tulle and garlanded evening gown listening to some attentive youth whispering sweet nothings about her delicacy and charm. Your long-distance swimmer can be the most gracious hostess in the world in a trailing teagown. The young girl who swings a golf club with amazing proficiency will suddenly surprise you with her flair for music. The clear-eyed young goddess whose airplane defies an angry storm to wrest it from life and safety, will tell you calmly how much she likes to cook and make her own clothes....

—Carol Cameron. "Who and What Is the Modern Girl?"
Physical Culture magazine, 1934

LOVE, and SU...
My "Fifty-

58

OVER THE FENCE IS OUT

A STEAL

A SACRIFICE

Catching a hot one

Covering left field

Now the other dames
of bygone fame
had best stay in the rear;
The modern dame
has made a name
that'll cling for many years;
With talents rare,
no one will dare
to challenge her to fray,
She's got the skill, also a will
to win whate'er she plays;
A bowler too, her aim is true
at gunning on the green;
Excels at cards,
a hundred yards
she dashes like a hare,
She'll dance or sing,
does everything but swear.
—Song lyric, "The College Girl," 1903

She is the Queen of the Bicycle Girls!
She is the Queen of The Bicycle Girls!
Cool as an icicle, when on her bicycle,
She down the boulevard whirls.
My little bicycle girl,
Of all the maids she's the pearl,
Come now with me, and you shall see
My little bicycle girl.

—Song lyric, "Queen of the Bicycle Girls,"
by W. H. Gardner, 1897

MAY ALLEN

on her Peerless ....

60

לשנה טובה תכתב
A happy New Year

We're taking a Flying
Visit to
BRIGHTON.

HAVING A HIGH OLD TIME.

לשנה טובה תכתבו
A happy New Year

61

BELLES-ARTES

Taste is the feminine of genius.
—Edward Fitzgerald, 1877

These charming dryads in a grove of eucalyptus trees are students of Mills College, participating in a recent outdoor festival at that California institution—the only woman's college on the Pacific Slope. They are posing beside the waters of a beautiful little lake on their campus, which is one of the many features of a State to which Nature has been unusually generous.

FINE ART

A REMBRANDT THOUGH I'LL NEVER BE,
MY WORK IS REALLY CLASSY.
BUT HIS ATTRACTION WON'T COMPARE;
HE DIDN'T HAVE MY CHASSIS.

The faculties of which genius is composed are precisely those in which women are deficient by nature. They may prove themselves ingenious, touching, and even eloquent in the most elevated regions of art—rarely <u>superior</u>. By compensation, or, rather, in consequence of that law, they ought to excel in elegiac poetry, in romance, in epistolary effort, and in conversation. In the last two, indeed, they are, and should be, beyond the reach of masculine emulation. Here their very defects become qualities of success.

—William H. Walling, A.M., M.D.,
Sexology, Philadelphia, 1904

"His Master's Voice"

67

THE WORKING GIRL

City Girl
Country Girl
Servant Girl

How would you like my job?

"Woman's place is in the home." It certainly has been; but she has also had a place in the factory, the office, the shop, the schoolroom, and the hospital, as these pictures show. Women, in fact, have always been a large part of the work force in the United States. In 1900, twenty percent of all wage earners were female; today, over forty percent are.

In colonial days and when the nation was young, there was a serious shortage of labor. Women, like everyone else, old and young, were expected to work hard. And they did, at just about every kind of work that had to be done. After the Civil War, as the country became industrialized and urbanized, more and more women went to work outside the home for wages, but they were restricted to "women's work."

Throughout the century after the war, most women were denied vocational training, higher education, and access to professional skills, and women's work generally was unskilled, menial labor. Women labored mainly as clerks, typists, saleswomen, farm hands, domestic servants, and operators in garment and textile factories. The most prestigious jobs commonly available to them were in nursing and teaching, which seemed peculiarly appropriate to women and an extension of their traditional domestic functions. Women, it was assumed, were specially fitted to care for and instruct young children (not college students). After the Civil War, when teaching became professionalized, special teacher-training schools were established to which women were admitted, and teaching became an exception, a skilled job available to women. Nonetheless, in teaching, as in all other jobs, women consistently earned less than men, often receiving one-half to one-third men's pay for the same work. Moreover, in all their fields of employment there was little room for advancement. Management positions were considered men's work. In schools, although the vast majority of the teachers were female, supervisors and principals as well as school boards were overwhelmingly male until very recently. Everywhere, clear-cut lines separated men's work from women's work.

Nowhere is the gap between popular images of women and the realities of their lives greater than in the case of working women. In these pictures, working looks almost like play. With few exceptions, the wage earner is a pretty young girl, smilingly employed at a pleasant, light task. For her, employment is clearly fun. She is neither strong, serious, nor sweaty as she toils. Indeed, her work often is portrayed as a chance to meet handsome young men or flirt with the boss.

In truth, until our own times, most of the women who went into the work force were poor women who labored because they had to. Until World War II, the female work force was made up primarily of immigrant women and their daughters and black women. Ununionized, unskilled, generally unprotected by laws, their working experiences often were chronicles of horror. They were the poorest-paid workers in the land; they labored sixty and seventy hours a week in laundries, in kitchens, in private homes, in shops, on farms, and in filthy and dangerous factories. Against the reality of their lives, the smiling faces on these pages can only seem ironic!

Since the era of World War II, many changes have occurred for working women. More married, older, and middle-class women have sought employment than ever before. By the 1960s and 1970s, women were slowly gaining access to better jobs and professions. Increased numbers of women workers had been unionized, and neither unions nor employers could legally discriminate against them. For the first time in American history, the principle of equal pay for equal work was written directly into the law, and equal educational and vocational opportunities were, on paper at least, now available to women. And although women workers are still the least skilled and the poorest paid in the work force, the working woman today has advantages unknown to her predecessors.

THE
WORKING GIRL

CITY GIRL

How can I, a woman absolutely without previous
experience, earn the money so necessary to the welfare and
happiness of myself and those I love?
This is a question thousands of women are asking themselves every
day. They have a vital need for more money—to help support
a family—to pay off a mortgage or buy a home—to educate their children
or to pay doctor's bills—to tide over war times—there
are many reasons why.

—Advertisement, World's Star
Knitting Company, 1917

OUR SALESLADY

A PAIR OF CLIPPERS

OH, I HAVE A "CINCH"

Boss Lady

1066. The Model—Getting Ready for the Pose.

NUN NICER

GROUP OF DEMONSTRATORS, WALTER BAKER & CO., LTD.

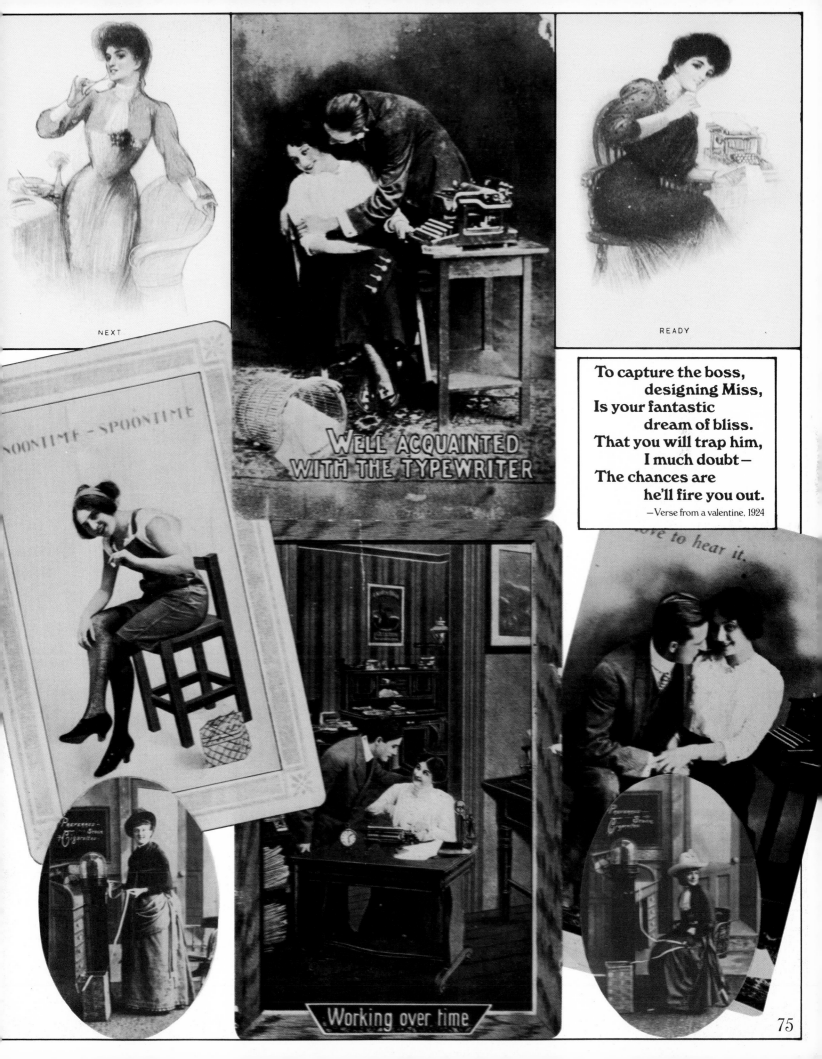

NEXT

READY

WELL ACQUAINTED WITH THE TYPEWRITER

NOONTIME - SPOONTIME

To capture the boss,
    designing Miss,
Is your fantastic
    dream of bliss.
That you will trap him,
    I much doubt—
The chances are
    he'll fire you out.

—Verse from a valentine, 1924

Working over time

J. DUNCAN GLEASON

THE MAXFIELD PA

The dining-room, in which 500 girls can lunch at one time in the new home of THE LADIES' HOME JOURNA
on the next page. It is spoken of as "the most beautiful dining-room in America."
a hundred steps from the historic Independence Hall with its

RISH DINING-ROOM

w open. It is called "The Maxfield Parrish Dining-Room" because of Mr. Parrish's beautiful panels described

URNAL'S new home is now open for visitors. It is directly facing Independence Square:

iberty Bell. When you come to see the Bell come and see us.

How _American_ it is...to want something better!

SURE this war-plant worker looks forward to "something better"—resuming study for her chosen career, that long-planned trip or to marriage.

That's why she's putting a healthy part of her earnings into war bonds and stamps—to speed the return of peace and all the other things which help make this "the land of something better."

Some of us can help most in the front lines, others on production lines—_all_ of us can buy war bonds and stamps!

78

They're running farmer's tractors—
they're at a factory bench—
The hands that rock the cradle
wield a nifty monkey wrench.

They're wearing pants and jumpers
made of denims and of drills—
And the dirndlest-looking dirndls
made of sturdy cotton twills.

—Advertisement, "Sanforized." 1942

She's 5 feet 1 from her **4A** slippers to her spun-gold hair. She loves flower-hats, veils, smooth orchestras—and being kissed by a boy who's now in North Africa.

But, man, oh man, how she can handle her huge and heavy press!

Wait a minute....How can 110 pounds of beauty boss 147,000 pounds of steel?...Is this magic?

Yes, in a way. The modern magic of electric power. The magic that makes it possible for a girl's slim fingers to lift mountains of metal, or set great wheels in motion—just by pressing a button or pulling a lever.

Women are able to work beside men on America's roaring production lines because electricity does the heavy labor.

—"Woman Power," advertisement sponsored by 114 electric companies as part of war effort. 1943

Your Friend
THE NURSE

For the Industrial Policy-hold
Metropolitan Life Insurance

Save his life…
and find your own
BE A NURSE

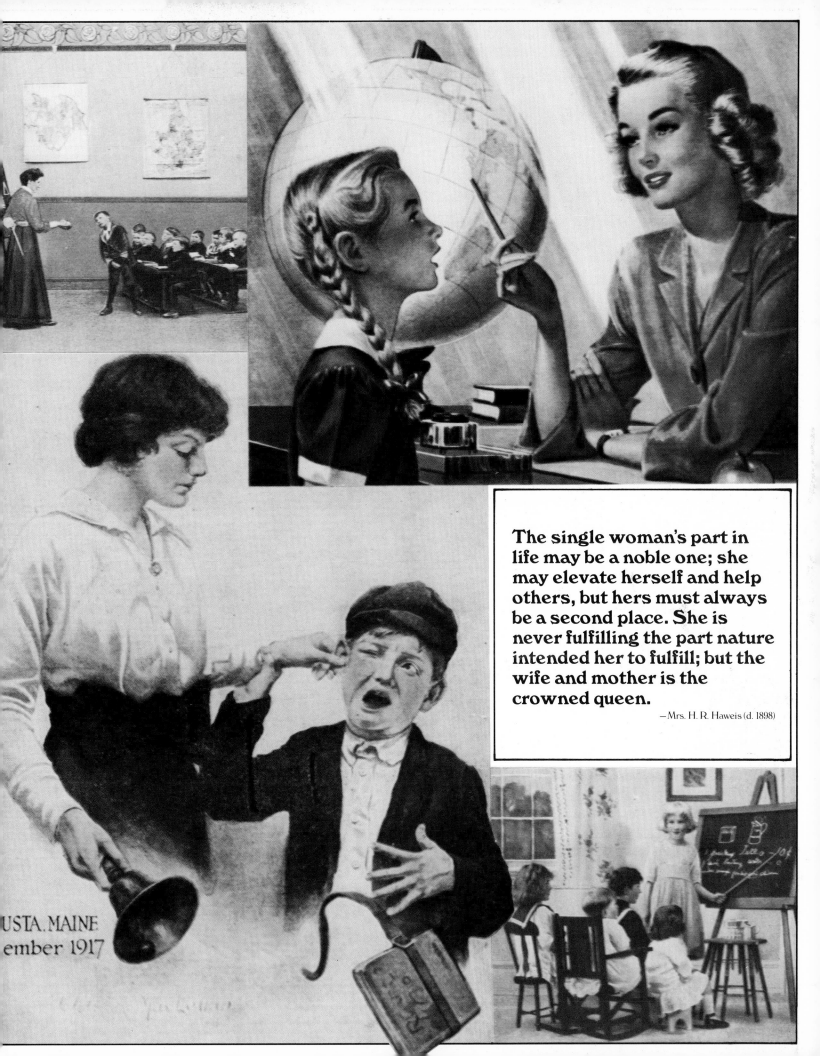

The single woman's part in life may be a noble one; she may elevate herself and help others, but hers must always be a second place. She is never fulfilling the part nature intended her to fulfill; but the wife and mother is the crowned queen.

—Mrs. H. R. Haweis (d. 1898)

THE WORKING GIRL

COUNTRY GIRL

The Most Resourceful Woman in the World. She is a good cook, a good dressmaker, a good housekeeper, but more than that. She knows how to raise flowers, vegetables, chickens and bees; how to milk, churn and can. She is the wife of the most important man in the world and is the mother of the men who have made America. She is the American Farmer's Wife.

—Advertisement, The Country Gentleman, 1917

THE SHARPLES TUBULAR SEPARATOR

FARM PLEASURES

WEST CHESTER, PA.

"A PEACH OF A LOAD."

The Dairy Maid

84

THE WORKING GIRL

SERVANT GIRL

To feel, to love,
to suffer, to devote
herself will
always be the text
of the life of
a woman.

— Honoré de Balzac (1799-1850)

Sarah has a "repitashun" for fried chicken. As nearly as Mrs. Clark can spell the rich, golden brown words of that jewel among cooks, Sarah Said:

"Firs ah cuts de cheekin in pieces. Den ah puts Snowdrif in de pan and when it's hot ah puts in de pieces a cheekin which ah has prevously dipped in melk en rolled in flour."

"No one in the world like mammy"

AMERICAN BEAUTY

Dream Girl
Vanity Fair

Every woman in this chapter is beautiful and young—as is almost every woman in this book—although humanity, female as well as male, comes in many forms, lean and lumpy, stringy and dumpy, weathered and wrinkled, pitted and puckered. Still in the popular imagery, as well as in poetry, novels, and films, most women are beautiful. There are many varieties of female beauty; it can be exotic or wholesome, innocent or seductive. Tastes change from era to era. But feminine beauty is always found in a woman's face and body. The beautiful woman is an object, a decorative, lovely thing.

In the twentieth century, an enormous industry developed that offered every woman the chance to attain beauty. At the turn of the century, women who painted themselves were still considered promiscuous; respectable women might timidly touch up with a bit of rice flour. By the 1920s, however, the cosmetic industry had convinced men and women alike that primping, painting, and powdering were morally sound and that looking lovely was part of a woman's responsibility.

Being beautiful became simple: a woman had only to buy the right product to stay young, to have skin as smooth as a baby's, hair that was a crowning glory, perfect teeth, a desirable figure, and to smell like the rose she was. The woman in search of beauty was the seller's dream because she consumed his products in order to be what she was supposed to be. Fighting against time and changing fashions, she became the perpetual buyer.

As with other material things, the value of women increases as their beauty increases; the loveliest are the costliest. The most beautiful women can be seen in the most expensive restaurants and shops, as possessions of rich and powerful men. A man's woman, like his automobile, is a symbol of status and achievement. He underwrites her efforts to be beautiful, no matter how high the cost, because her beauty reflects on him. A good-looking gal, as the saying goes, can go far. This is the fantasy. Yet everyone knows that few men are rich enough to own a woman as a beautiful object. Usually a wife is a household manager, a cleaner and a cook, a child rearer, a social secretary, a nurse and chauffeur, a partner in sex, and often an auxiliary wage earner. Intelligence, sensitivity, a head for numbers, a sense of order, kindness, a healthy interest in sex—these are her real qualifications for marriage.

Why, then, the fantasy and the imagery that take the real woman out of her shell, glorify the shell, and ignore the woman? The emphasis on physical attributes in women contrasts sharply with the emphasis on intelligence, talent, and creativity as male attributes. Equating female perfection with physical beauty results in a view of women as less intelligent and able than men; and it lies at the root of their inferior status in American life.

Fantasies about female beauty have had profound effects on both men and women. No man would pick an old flower or a common weed from the garden when he could have a rose. And dying on the vine was a real danger to many women who could not support themselves or lead a fulfilled life without a man to take care of them. Consequently women have focused on their appearance. They have cracked their ribs to have small waists; they have tottered perilously on high heels; they have shaved their bodies, teased their hair, starved their bellies, flattened their breasts or pumped them with silicone. Those who deviated too far from the current popular image to hope to conform suffered a loss of self-esteem and the pain of rejection. Behind the fantasy of the American Beauty rose lies a harsh and bitter reality.

American Beauty
DREAM GIRL

Girl of my dreams — the garden of roses
Brings back memories of you,
Beautiful eyes of blue,
hair of a golden hue,
You're fresh as the morning dew,
Girl of my dreams.

—Song lyric, "Girl of My Dreams," 1920. Copyright 1920. Renewed by Harry Tobias.

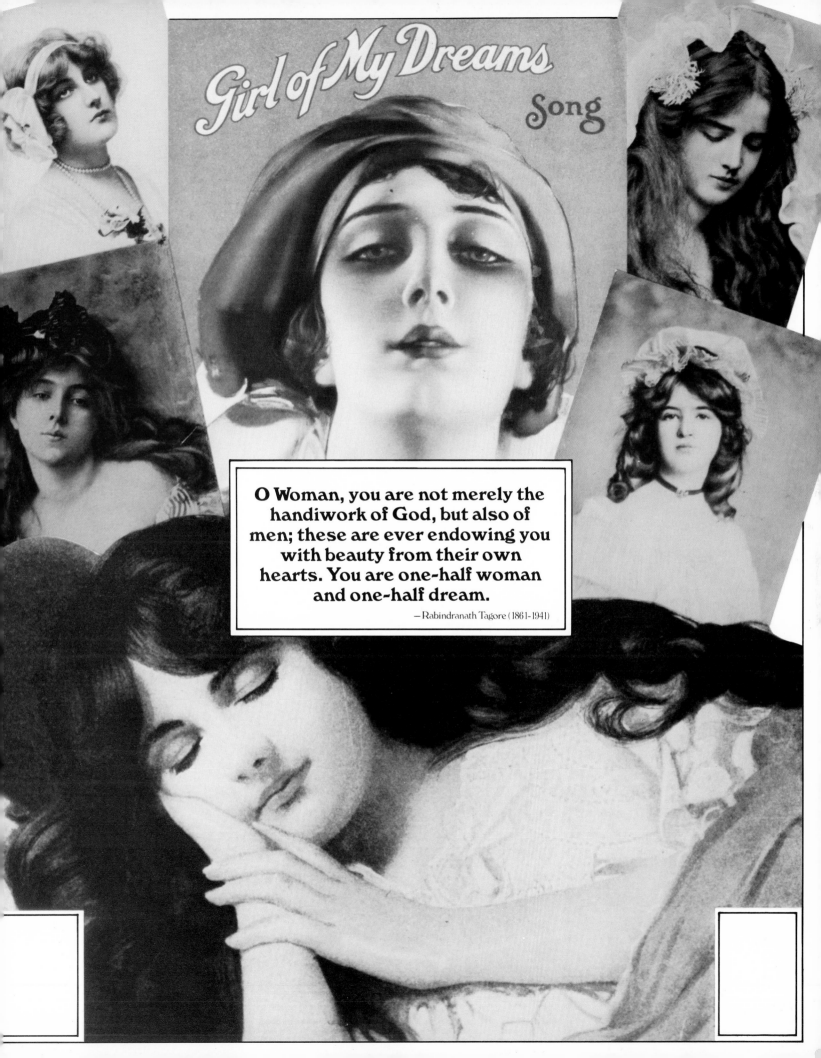

O Woman, you are not merely the handiwork of God, but also of men; these are ever endowing you with beauty from their own hearts. You are one-half woman and one-half dream.

—Rabindranath Tagore (1861-1941)

There is a garden in her face
Where roses and
White lilies blow;
A heav'nly paradise is that place
Wherein all pleasant
Fruits do grow.

—Thomas Campion, c. 161

96

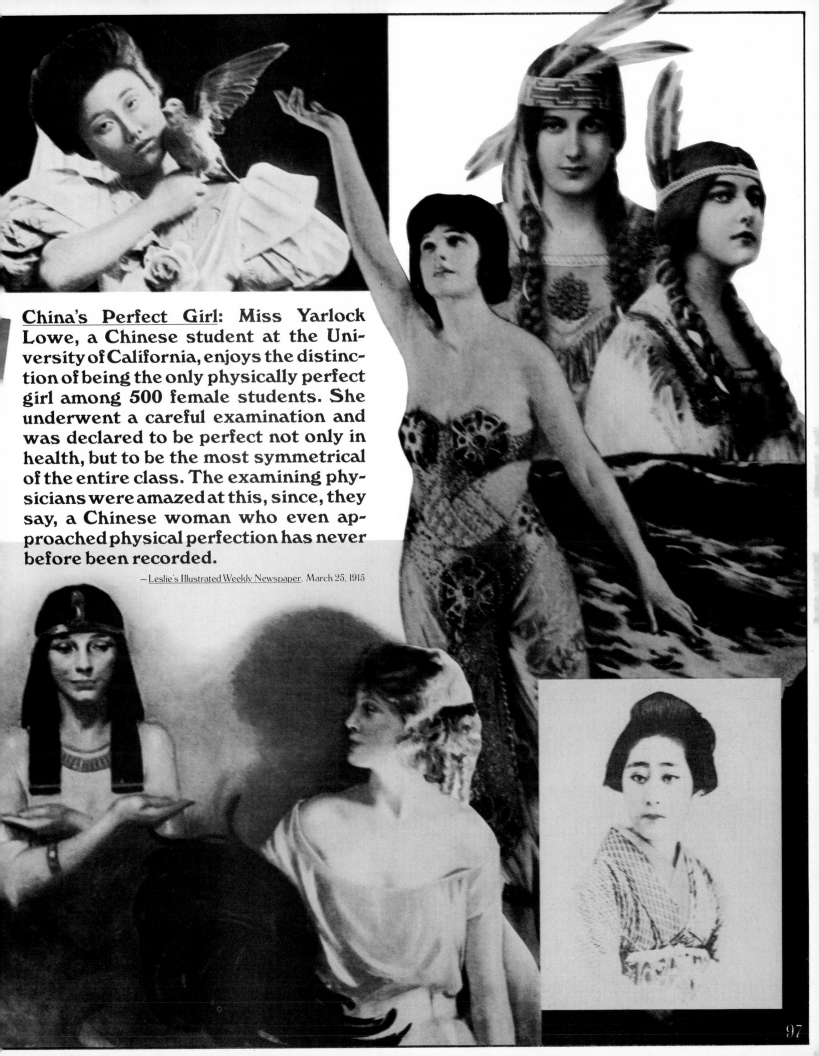

China's Perfect Girl: Miss Yarlock Lowe, a Chinese student at the University of California, enjoys the distinction of being the only physically perfect girl among 500 female students. She underwent a careful examination and was declared to be perfect not only in health, but to be the most symmetrical of the entire class. The examining physicians were amazed at this, since, they say, a Chinese woman who even approached physical perfection has never before been recorded.

—Leslie's Illustrated Weekly Newspaper. March 25, 1915

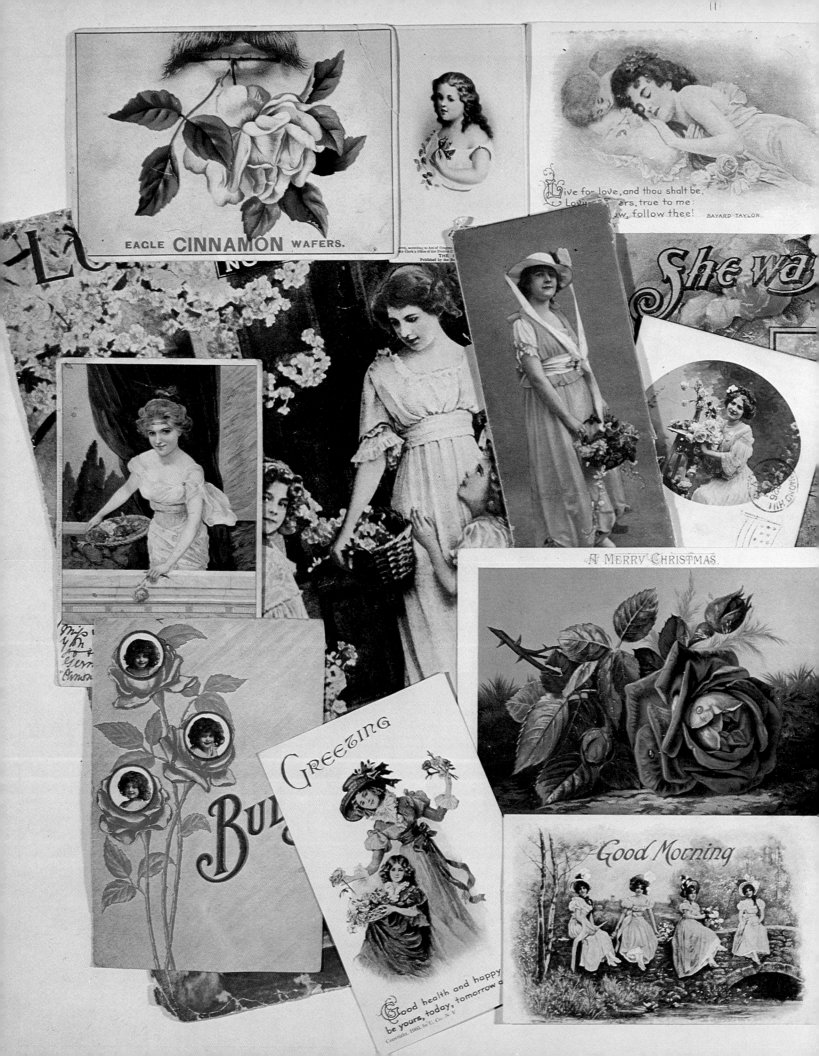

To Woman

"fairest of creation,
last and best!" MILTON
t. 1905. by U. Co. N. Y.

Rosebud

Musical Supplement to the New York Sunday Press

Sunday, D

LIBRARY OF
WILLIAM J. McKENNA
NO.

Pretty Kitty

SINCERE WISHES

AT THE OPERA

She did not heed the lessons
that she learned at mother's knee,
Her life was young,
and pleasure rul'd the hour;
She met the one who tempted her,
his bride she thought to be,
And left the home of which
she was the flow'r.

She was a rosebud in bloom
when last I met her.
Her girlish face has changed so
since that day.
No matter how I try,
I can't forget her,
She's a blossom that
is fading fast away.

—Song lyric, "She Was a Rosebud." 1898

AMERICAN
BEAUTY

VANITY FAIR

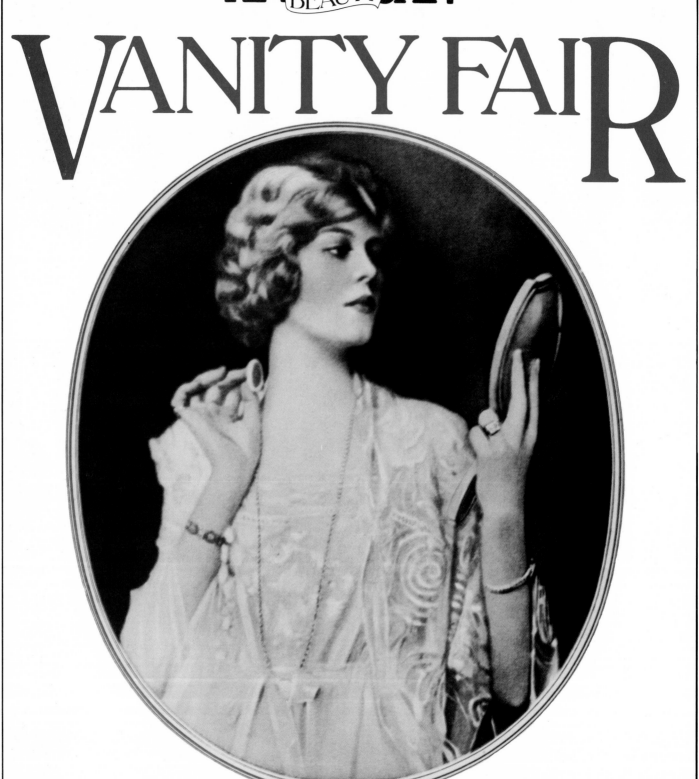

**Mirror, mirror on the wall
Who's the fairest of them all?**

— "Snow White and the Seven Dwarfs"

Most men ask "Is she pretty?" not "Is she clever?"

Beauty Wins—Beauty Keeps

The secret of keeping beauty lies in keeping that schoolgirl complexion, as millions know who follow this simple daily rule:

BEAUTY is not mere regularity of features, or a shade of hair. It is an ensemble in which a good complexion plays a vital part.

Many otherwise unattractive girls have "lovely eyes," or "a good nose." And many girls are called beautiful whose greatest claim to beauty is a lovely skin.

To be *really* pretty one must keep her natural charm. For even though you use powder and rouge, *naturalness* is your aim. And no beauty can seem natural that has not the base of a naturally lovely skin.

Those authorities who know the most of dermatology—of skin culture—will tell you "washing the face for beauty" is Nature's surest rule.

Wash with lather of these famed beauty oils—daily

The soothing, cleansing oils of olive and palm, as embodied in the famous beauty soap, Palmolive, are recommended, if natural beauty is what you seek.

These gentle cleansers soothingly penetrate the pores, remove accumulations which, if left, would form into blackheads, or, becoming infected, would cause unsightly blemishes.

They bring the charm of natural loveliness because they keep the skin cleansed *Nature's* way. To keep that schoolgirl complexion through the years, do this at least once daily.

Do this for one week, then note results

Wash your face gently with soothing Palmolive Soap, massaging its balmy lather softly into the skin with your two hands. Rinse thoroughly, first with warm water, then with cold. Dry by patting with a soft towel—never rub the gentle skin fabric.

If your skin is inclined to be dry, apply a touch of good cold cream—that is all. Do this regularly, and particularly in the evening. Use powder and rouge if you wish. But never leave them on over night.

And Palmolive costs but 10c the cake! So little that millions let it do for their bodies what it does for their faces. Obtain a cake today, then note the difference one week makes. The Palmolive-Peet Company, Chicago, Ill.

PALMOLIVE

3905

Retail Price

10c

Palmolive Soap is untouched by human hands until you break the wrapper—it is never sold unwrapped

KEEP THAT SCHOOLGIRL COMPLEXION

For him... and him... and him...

"I pledge myself to guard every bit of Beauty that he cherishes in me"

The importance of our faces to us can not be estimated. They are our fortunes indeed. They make us friends, or enemies. There is no telling when our faces are going to bring, or take from us, good fortune, love, riches, adventure.

—Elsie Ferguson, "Your Face Is Your Fortune," Woman's World, 1921

Will Your Hair Stand Close Inspection?

Is it soft and silky, bright and fresh looking — full of life and lustre?

YOUR hair, more than anything else, makes or spoils your whole appearance.

It tells the world what you are.

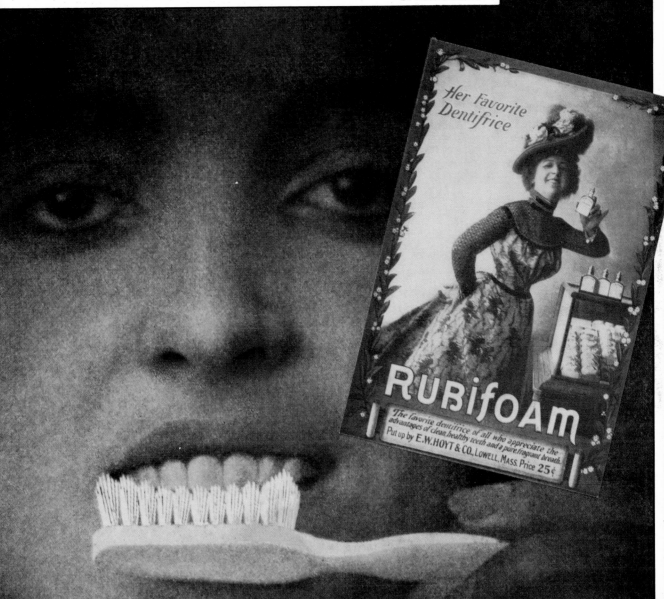

**The milk-white pearls of the necklace
which she wore were excelled in purity by her teeth.**

—Sir Walter Scott, 1821

Her Favorite Dentifrice

RUBifoaM

The favorite dentifrice of all who appreciate the
advantages of clean healthy teeth and a pure fragrant breath.
Put up by E.W. HOYT & CO., LOWELL, MASS. Price 25¢

**Some ask'd how pearls did grow, and where?
Then spoke I to my girl,
To part her lips, and shew'd them there
The quarelets of pearl.**

—Robert Herrick, "The Rock of Rubies
and Quarrie of Pearls" (quoted in
Colgate Dental Cream advertisement, 1921)

A beautiful and chaste woman is
the perfect workmanship of God,
the true glory of the angels,
the rare miracle of earth,
and the sole wonder of the world.

—Georg Hermes (1775-1831)

In her hand this dainty nurse
The symbolism bears,
Of Purity and Excellence
And Cleanliness – 'tis PEARS'

SANITARY MAID

Purity

The LILY is the Symbol of Natural Purity—CLEANLINESS
If Nature were to undertake our Washing and Cleaning for us—
PEARLINE and PEARLINE'S method would be the means used.

Pearline Possesses Peculiar Purifying Properties
—besides in doing away with the rubbing it DOES AWAY with
the worst of the Work and Wear and Tear.

"This *can't* apply to me!"

A RATHER unusual advertisement had caught her eye and set her wondering. It talked about something she had never heard discussed among the people she knew—not even the most intimate of her girl acquaintances.

But it set her thinking.

Maybe this was the thing that was holding her back with the men she wanted most to attract—a thing that had never before entered her mind.

* * *

That's the insidious thing about halitosis (unpleasant breath). You, yourself, rarely know when you have it. And even your closest friends won't tell you.

Sometimes, of course, halitosis comes from some deep-seated organic disorder that requires professional advice. But usually—and fortunately—halitosis is only a local condition that yields to the regular use of Listerine as a mouth wash and gargle. It is an interesting thing that this well-known antiseptic that has been in use for years for surgical dressings, possesses these unusual properties as a breath deodorant.

It halts food fermentation in the mouth and leaves the breath sweet, fresh and clean. *Not* by substituting some other odor but by really removing the old one. The Listerine odor itself quickly disappears. So the systematic use of Listerine puts you on the safe and polite side.

Your druggist will supply you with Listerine. He sells lots of it. It has dozens of different uses as a safe antiseptic and has been trusted as such for half a century. Read the interesting little booklet that comes with every bottle. —*Lambert Pharmacal Company, Saint Louis, U. S. A.*

107

It is no more sin in a woman to thank God for the fair looks and pretty clothing which enable her to delight others, than it is for a man to thank God for his accumulation of money, and his ability to use it in making others happy.

—Amelia E. Barr, "Happiness and Dress," 1899

The Live Model Corset

Special 35th Anniversary Values

For every type of figure

Ask your dealer for KABO Anniversary Corsets designed and fitted over Live Models to give perfect style and entire comfort sitting or standing. Guaranteed not to rust, tear or break. Ask for

KABO No. 4099 at $5.00
KABO No. 2099 at $3.00
KABO No. 4039 at $2.00

KABO Brassieres Special Anniversary values at $1 to $4. Send for our Beautiful KABO Style Book.

Perfect Health Corset Superior to all Others

KABO CORSET CO.
NEW YORK, CHICAGO, SAN FRANCISCO.

"Perfect"

American Lady

No wonder she's alone.
But who's to blame for that.
He thought it was a rose bush.
That MERRY WIDOW HAT.

I CAN'T KICK.--

An American's wife is the peg on which he hangs out his fortune; he dresses her up that men may see his wealth; she is a walking advertisement of his importance. The Englishman loves his house and decks it out when he makes money; the American loves his wife and decks her out for want of a house.

—James Stirling, 1850

COURTIN' 'N' SPOONIN'

Love
...And Marriage

> **Love, which is only an episode in the life of a man,
> is the entire history of woman's life.**
> —Madame de Staël (1766–1817)

Courtin' and spoonin' look like fun, lighthearted games played by coy women and pursuing men. Their depiction in these pages reflects increasing social and sexual freedom since the Civil War. For the sex play portrayed here is not limited to courtship and, by association, to marriage; spooning is also acceptable social behavior, and good women can indulge in sexual banter outside of marriage without condemnation.

However, the shadow of Victorianism is still visible everywhere, and courting as well as spooning is limited to "the outposts of virginity." There are few suggestions here of women openly and robustly interested in sex for its own pleasures. Instead a quasi-sexuality is depicted, characterized by teasing and suggestiveness. The women have something men want; they are keepers of the gate, guardians of a treasure. The game they play is an odd prelude to sex or to marriage.

Most of the spooning is linked to marriage, as diamond rings and wedding bands hover over the cavorting couples. For women, getting married has usually been the most important step in life. It gave them a new name and legal status, a new home, new responsibilities and obligations, and society's permission to have children without censure. Few women in the nineteenth century did not get married. Marriage was virtually obligatory for them, and for men too, although to a lesser degree. Single women, it was thought, went against God's will—and man's. They often suffered scorn and embarrassment and usually lived in poverty, unable to support themselves comfortably with decent jobs. Even in the early 1900s, as the number of unmarried women increased (at first among college-educated women), a single woman was still an oddity, a nonconformist in a society based on the assumption that women were programmed by God, nature, and biology to be mothers and therefore, necessarily, to be wives.

How strange then that courtship, the process of finding a marriage partner, is most frequently depicted as a lighthearted game. One could hardly surmise that it really was a prelude to the serious business of marriage, a contractual arrangement involving both parties in an exchange of economic and sexual duties and obligations, carefully defined by both law and tradition and, until recently, very difficult to dissolve.

The idea of marrying for love dominates the imagery of courtship. Before the nineteenth century, financial considerations, geographical restrictions, social customs, and parental authority combined to limit young people's freedom in choosing mates. But as society changed, free choice became more common. With choice, love rushed in on the scene. Although it had been part of Western tradition for a long time, in its earlier manifestations love had played a minor role in marriage. As courtly love, it could only occur outside of marriage, and as romantic love, it was usually the province of the upper classes. By the twentieth century, love had been democratized and domesticated. While our Puritan forefathers cautioned couples not to love too much, lest they lose sight of God and their duties to him, in our time one cannot love too much. Love has become the popular and dominant rationale for marriage, and under its spell, courtship overwhelms the realities of married life that follow upon its heels, and myth prevails.

COURTIN' 'N SPOONIN'
LOVE

She halts his ardent demonstration
Elusive maid! What aggravation!
He falls to Cupid's fascination
Aided by her coy flirtation.

—Postcard verse, 1905

MY WIFE'S GONE TO THE COUNTRY

WILL SHOW YOU HOW.

Oh, you Candy Kid.

NOBODY to LOVE

I AM LOOKING FOR YOU

Man Wanted.

TO LET

I'm a little wallflower
      blooming alone.
I've never known a heart
      I could call my own.
Nobody to love—
I'm wondering why
The ones I could love
Keep passing me by.
I've got a heart full of loving
That's just going to waste
But for reasons unknown
I am always alone.
I've studied the books
On winning a heart
But nobody looks
So how can I start?
I've been so long
      all alone on the shelf
I'll soon be hating myself.
I'm growing so weary of
Having nobody to love.

—Song lyric, "Nobody to Love," 1920

I can't resist you, sir,
When your instrument you play
With your rooty tooty tooty
On your tricky little fluty
Charmed my little heart away.

—Song lyric, "The Band Song," 1904

Everybody's doing it

Hang it any way—It's a Kiss

May you always be in a position to help yourself

A CREAM SEPARATOR

KISS ME KID AND KNOW YOU'RE LIVING

"*I* do"

"It's toasted"

LUCKY STRIKE "IT'S TOASTED" CIGARETTES

...AND MARRIAGE

Dearest, I'll skip away to town,
Dearest, I'll buy a wedding gown,
You go tell the preacher to be ready when we call,
Then, how happy we will be
When it's all reality.
Can you imagine just a cozy little cottage,
Can you imagine one just built for you and me,
Where roses bloom, dear,
In the morning, night and noon, dear,
And birdies chirp pretty tunes of love.

—Song lyric, "Can You Imagine," 1919

"ASK MOTHER."

"DEARIE, WON'T YOU MARRY ME"

Let's elope.

HOW MEN PROPOSE.

IN THE "OLE PLANTATION"

"SPEAK FOR IT!"

I'D BUY DIAMONDS FOR YOU.

forever
and ever..

124

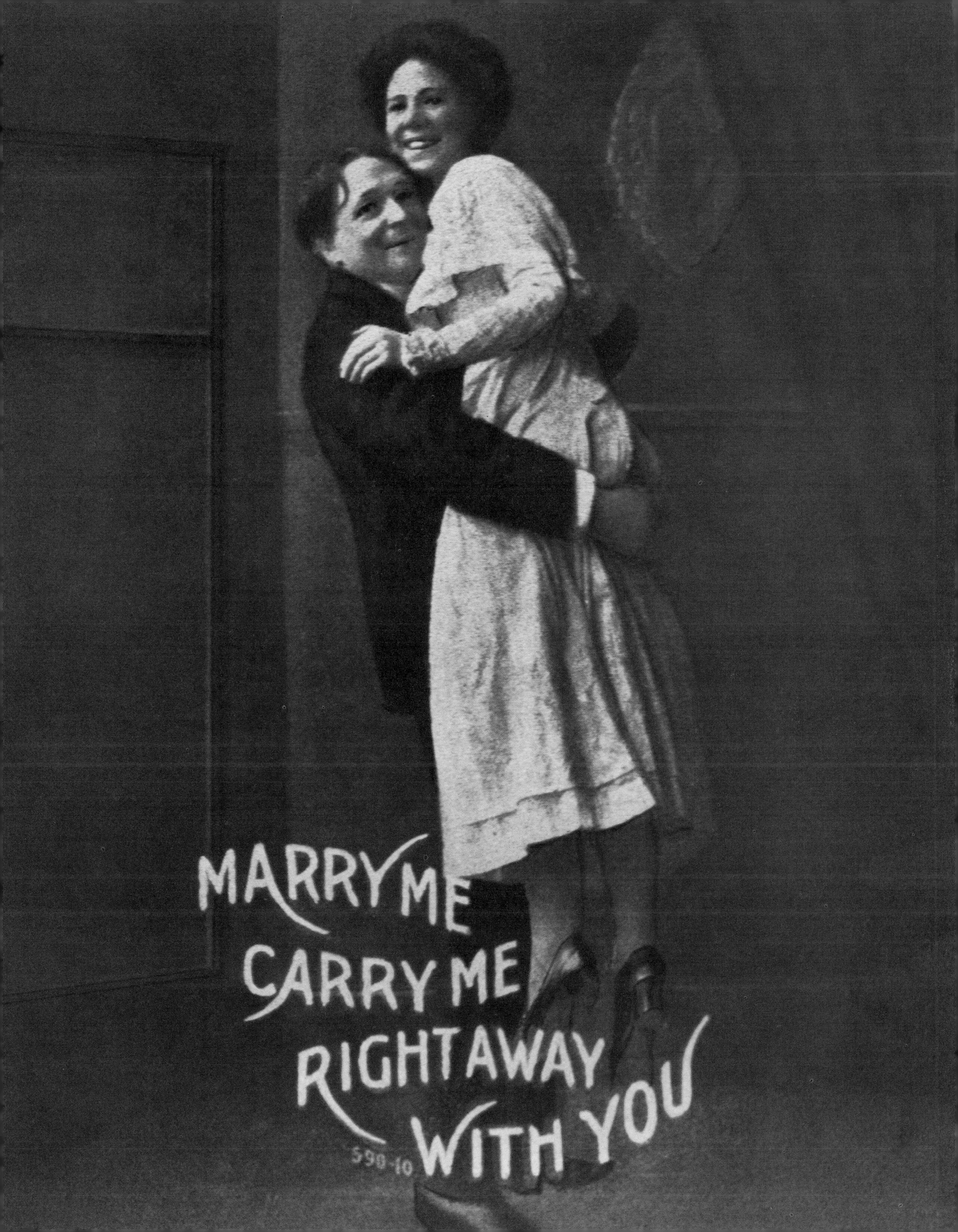
MARRY ME
CARRY ME
RIGHT AWAY
WITH YOU
590-10

Purity of heart is the noblest inheritance, and love the fairest ornament of women.

—Matthias Claudius (1740-1815)

THE BRIDE.

"No Ring? Here's your Life Saver"

THIS IS NO LIBERTY BOND

"How it feels to mere Man."

HONEY, DOES YOU LUB YO' MAN?

Mr
Mrs

"*–and so they lived
happily ever after*"

WOMAN'S PLACE IS IN THE HOME

Mother
Wife

What is Home without a Mother

> **Man may work from sun to sun,**
> **But woman's work is never done.**
> —Old saying

A man's home is his castle. A woman's home is almost always the place in which she works, without wages, as wife, child rearer, and housekeeper. Even women who labor in factories, offices, and schoolrooms have usually been expected to work at home as well. With few exceptions, men do not; this is woman's work.

Woman's place in the home is surrounded by more imagery and myth than any other aspect of her life. Love, the reason for marriage, paves the young girl's path toward housekeeping, and after the satin wedding, love not only lingers on but grows, providing the main motive for the labor she performs as wife. Her reward for caring for her husband lies in his pleasure in the pie she bakes and in her well-kept house and her satisfaction in serving the man she loves.

Housework, in this scheme of things, is fun! Cooking, cleaning, and sewing come naturally to women. Meanwhile, a plethora of manufactured products aid the housewife and make her chores even easier and more satisfying.

The pinnacle of woman's work in the home is in child rearing. Motherhood, in the popular imagery, is what women are all about, their natural function. Women give birth to beautiful babies whom they nurture with grace and ease until they become contented, happy children.

As with most myths about women, the reality is vastly different. Courtship often proves to be a poor and even harmful prelude to the realities of married life, and romance does not necessarily endure. Love is not always sufficient compensation for the daily and repetitive labor of the housewife. Since the 1880s, state laws have been modified to expand the reasons for divorce and to simplify the divorce procedure. In increasing numbers, women seek divorce because they are unhappy in marriage. Love has ended, and without it, they do not want the job of being a wife.

The job itself is usually very different from what is portrayed. Although modern technology and industry have created many products to lighten the housewife's burdens, housekeeping remains, as it has always been, hard and unending work. By the late 1800s, housewives no longer wove cloth, made soap, brewed beer, hauled water, or gathered food daily as they once had done. But contemporary studies of housework show that women with small children at home still work at least eight hours a day, seven days a week. They perform many traditional tasks as well as new ones, such as gardening and chauffeuring. Moreover, the modern housewife is the largest consumer in the economy, spending hours each week purchasing products for the entire family. As such she is the prime target of advertising. Ads tell her what she must buy to be successful. Housekeeping standards are pushed to historic heights by eager sellers. The shine on the floors symbolizes her worth as a human being. Glasses must sparkle, not to be clean or healthy, but to testify to her devotion and skill. The appearance of house, children, food on the table, and her husband's shirts all reflects upon a woman's ability.

Child rearing, too, is a far cry from the sublime job that is pictured in popular images. To their surprise and shame, many women discover themselves to be short of the patience and generosity that are supposed to come automatically with motherhood. Happy suckling babies may actually be miserable with colic. Curly-headed cherubs may be ornery and trying children. Although families have grown smaller with industrialization and urbanization, in other ways the business of raising children has grown more complex and demanding as our attitudes toward childhood have changed. Psychologists call it the critical period of life in which basic personality structure is set. Parents try to make it a secure and happy time. And the woman in particular bears the new and awesome responsibility of laying the foundations for the mental health and psychological well-being of the next generation. As wife, housekeeper, and mother, her reality is far from the ideal of the simple, easily contented, and always satisfied woman pictured in the home of the popular images.

The Finest Thing in the World

MOTHER

A tiny bud, whose flowers complete
May bloom to bless my waning years;
Oh, **MOTHERHOOD!** you hold a bliss
That best may be expressed in tears.

— To Mothers, and Those Expecting to Become Mothers, Booklet, 1887

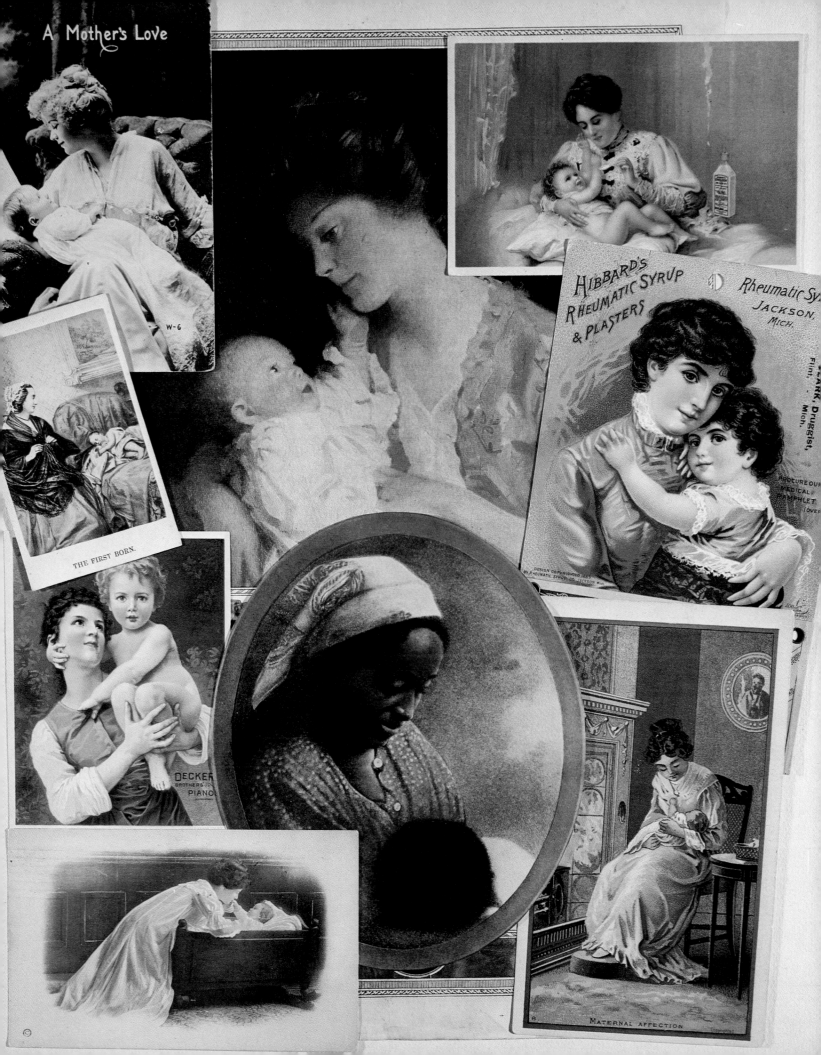

A Mother's Love

W-6

THE FIRST BORN.

DECKER BROTHERS PIANO

HIBBARD'S RHEUMATIC SYRUP & PLASTERS

Rheumatic Syrup

JACKSON, MICH.

MATERNAL AFFECTION

I hold a wee and helpless form
   Pressed closely to my happy
      heart—
Why, baby—mine by right divine—
   The right of pain—a mother's
      part.

Oh, beauteous life! so fair and
      new,
   That yesterday was blent with
      mine;
Oh, wondrous soul! so lately sprung
   A sparklet from the Source Divine.

God's priceless gift! you came to me
   Embodied in this little form;
My soul accepts its happiness
   As flowers the sunshine, soft
      and warm.

What realms are opened to my sight!
   I tread the regions of the blest;
And all because this little form
   Lies fair and helpless on my
      breast.

—"Motherhood," 1887 (anonymous)

God has placed the genius of women in their hearts; because the works of this genius are always works of love.

—Alphonse de Lamartine (1790-1869)

138

The hand that rocks the cradle
is the hand that sways the world,
In ev'ry land, no matter where
we roam;
And though we may be loyal
to our own dear native land,
Our hearts are true to Mother—
Queen of Home!

—Song lyric, "Mother, Queen of Home," 1899

WOMAN'S PLACE IS IN THE HOME

WIFE

The dignity of woman consists in being unknown to the world. — Her glory is the esteem of her husband; her pleasure the happiness of her family.

—Jean-Jacques Rousseau (1712-1778)

YOUR WIFE

FOR THIS
SHE GIVES UP EVRYTHING
A CROWN OF GOLD—
HER WEDDING RING!

LYRIC BY
ANDREW DONNELLY
AND
ADDISON BURKHARDT
MUSIC BY
AL. PIANTADOSI
WRITER OF
I DIDN'T RAISE MY BOY TO BE A SOLDIER
WHAT A WONDERFUL MOTHER YOU'D BE

Who is the one who sticks like glue
In sunshine and in rain,
Who'd scrape for you and scrub for you
And laugh away the pain?

Who is the one who
doesn't break the link,
Tho' from the path
You stray and take to drink?

It's your wife, it's your wife,
Who puts up with the strife,
When friends have
deserted she's true—
If things are going wrong
She cheers you with a song,
And looks happy tho'
Her heart is breaking too,
Don't forget, then regret,
That you owe her a debt,
She gave you the best part of her life,
And outside of your mother
There is only just one other
She's the noblest of sweethearts,
Your wife.
—Song lyric, "Your Wife." 1916 Copyright MCMXVI
by Shapiro, Bernstein & Co., Inc., New York. Renewed.

"I made it *all myself*"

Nothing equals the thrill of pride that comes from a fine baking of home-made bread made with your own hands to supply your own family table.

Do you make your husband happy?

Mrs. Dick: "I made them myself. I know they are kind of [b]onde—I know they cut like taffy—but, oh! Dick, I couldn't [he]lp it! I measured each ingredient just as carefully, and I [be]at everything together till my arm ached. And oh, I'm [so]rry—I thought pancakes would be such a surprise. I just [ca]n't tell how they are going to turn out—it's all luck."

Mr. Dick:
"Dearest, these pancakes are great! I could eat two dozen!"

The Hurry-Up Breakfast

How much of a man's fortune depends on his breakfast?
A good Breakfast, not too big, goes a long way toward making a man feel good.
When a man feels good he can do his best work.
Now it sometimes (not always) takes time to prepare a good breakfast.

The dear little wife at home, John,
With ever so much to do,
Stitches to set and babies to pet,
And so many thoughts of you—
The beautiful household fairy,
Filling your heart with light—
Whatever you meet today, John,
Go cheerily home tonight.

—Mary Lowe Dickinson, "The Dear Little Wife at Home," 1901

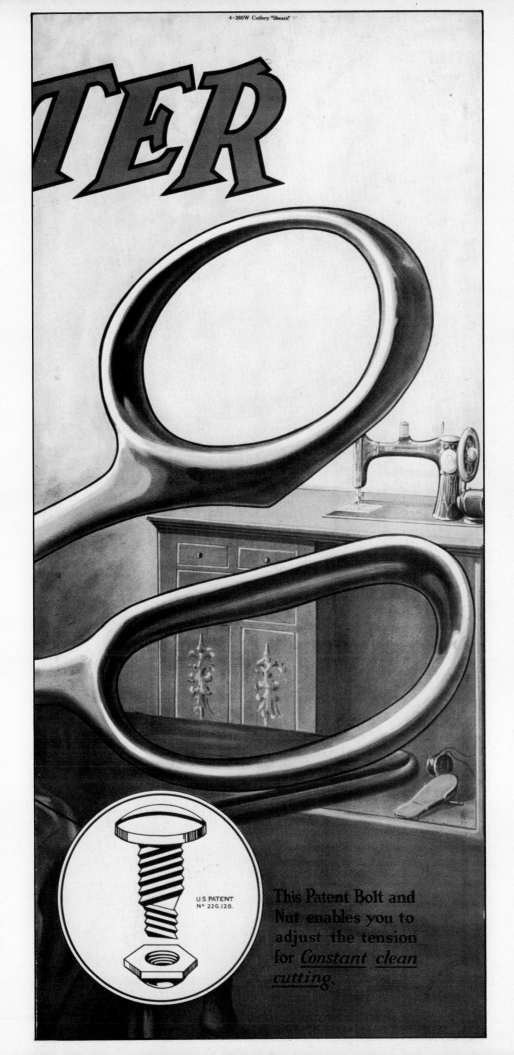

WINCHESTER
TRADE MARK
MADE IN U.S.A.

U.S. PATENT
Nº 226.128.

This Patent Bolt and Nut enables you to adjust the tension for *Constant clean cutting.*

145

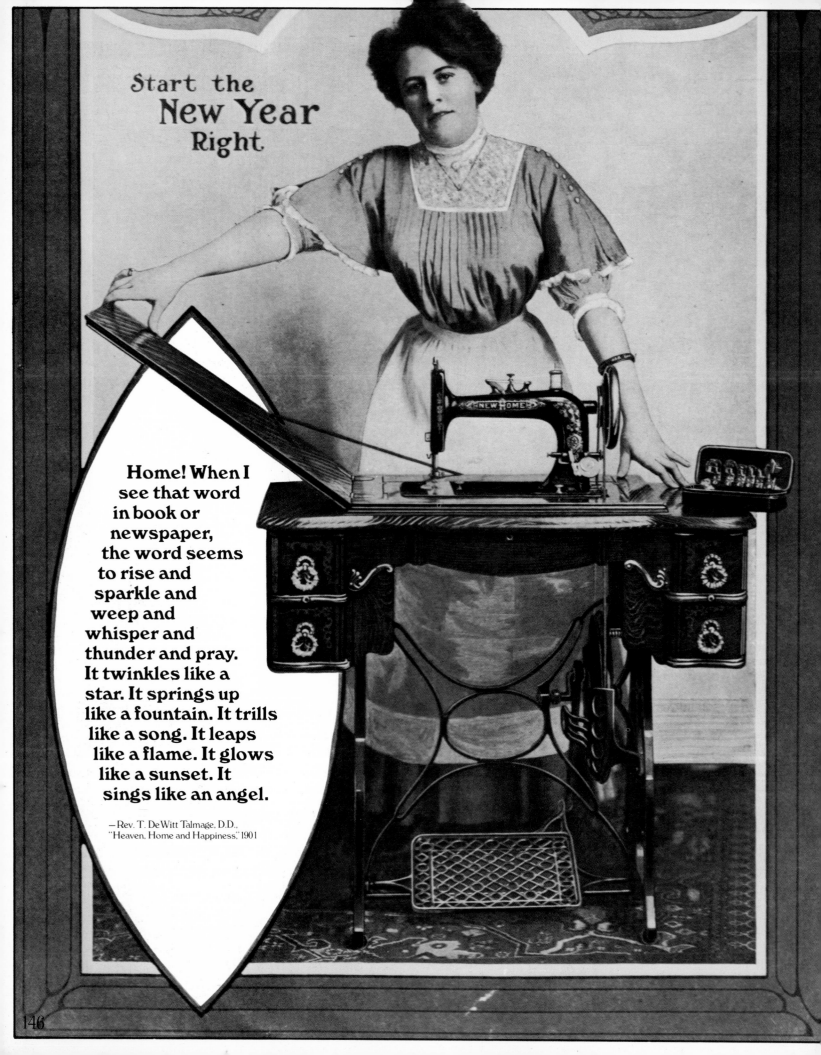

Start the
New Year
Right

Home! When I
see that word
in book or
newspaper,
the word seems
to rise and
sparkle and
weep and
whisper and
thunder and pray.
It twinkles like a
star. It springs up
like a fountain. It trills
like a song. It leaps
like a flame. It glows
like a sunset. It
sings like an angel.

—Rev. T. DeWitt Talmage, D.D.,
"Heaven, Home and Happiness," 1901

146

Hamilton Beach Vacuum Sweeper

Men come at eventide to the home; but all day long you are there, beautifying it, sanctifying it, adorning it, blessing it. Better be there than wear a queen's coronet. Better be there than carry the purse of a princess.

—Rev. T. De Witt Talmage, D.D., 1901

Women are doormats and have been—
The years these mats applaud—
They keep their men from going in
With muddy feet to God.

— Mary Carolyn Davies

House-Cleaning

Makes **Big Jobs** Look **Small**

Old Dutch Cleanser

Chases Dirt

MAKES EVERYTHING "SPICK AND SPAN"

Scrubs Scours Polishes

Happy Housecleaning!

AMERICA HURRAH!

America, I Love You

The Girl He Left Behind

Maidens in Uniform

**Here's to the Stars and Stripes—To the land of our birth
To the American Girl the best things on Earth.**

—Postcard verse, 1906

Sentimentality and idealism characterize the popular imagery of American life through all the decades included in <u>Myth America</u>. Children are angelic, women are gentle, homes are happy, men are strong, and justice is triumphant. In times of war, this idealization soars; the nation's myths are polished up and enlisted in the cause. So it is in the pictures in this chapter, which have been culled from the history of wartime America.

Modern warfare mobilizes not only soldiers and sailors but industrial workers and taxpayers as well. In industrialized societies, and especially in democracies, it is impossible to wage war without the support of most of the population. Elaborate techniques of education and communication are used to gain this support. War is sold: in effect, it becomes the ultimate product that everyone must buy in order to survive. The nation fights because the enemy threatens each one of us.

Thus, the pretty girl wrapped in the American flag transmits a complicated message: she is the girl next door; she is mother, grandmother, and all the defenseless persons who depend on men to protect them. She is family, home, and daily life. She is also Columbia, Liberty, and Justice. She is our way of life and the nation itself, which are in danger.

Throughout history, men have served as fighters, protectors, and hunters—strong, aggressive, and violent. Women have generally been the child rearers, the nurturers, and the protected—weak, passive, and gentle. Popular imagery consistently reflects and reinforces these differences; in wartime it underscores them. Women are even more passive than in peacetime. They urge their men to fight, tearfully send them off, and wait patiently for their return. When they serve directly in war activities, it is usually in a traditionally female way, as nurses caring for men.

Ironically, this emphasis on women's weakness and domesticity in wartime propaganda obscures what women have actually done and what war has meant to them. For every major American war has loosened the rigid role divisions that have consistently kept women out of productive and rewarding jobs in the economy and confined them to "women's work." During every war, a few women have actually disguised themselves as men and fought as soldiers. Most have stayed behind the lines to fill places vacated by men gone off to fight and to work at new jobs created by the war itself. During World War II, for example, women advanced into jobs in heavy manufacturing, government bureaucracy, and transportation, and even into some of the closed professional positions. Black women, normally confined to the least skilled and poorest-paying jobs such as laundry work, domestic service, and agricultural labor, moved into better-paying factory work in large numbers. In the 1940s, six million women who had not worked before joined the work force. The pattern had been set during the Civil War, and it has repeated itself with each successive wartime mobilization.

In the twentieth century, a new imagery developed in wartime to encourage women to bridge the gap between men's and women's work. It applauded women in uniforms and in pants. Rosie the Riveter, the WAC, and the WAVE were patriotic, admired, and, above all, still feminine. As long as the war lasted. But when the bands stopped playing and the emergency ended, they were expected to return to the kitchen, the nursery, the typing pool, and the schoolroom. Despite objections, for many women wanted to hold on to their good jobs, the nation returned to "normal life." That was, after all, what it had been fighting for in the first place.

AMERICA
HURRAH!
AMERICA,
I LOVE YOU

Three colors there are
in our banner,
And long they have floated
in pride,
From the ice of the North
to the tropics,
Fair Liberty's
beacon and guide.
They were born
in the heavens above us;
Every morning revives
them anew;
In the eyes, lips, and
cheeks of our maidens
Ever flourish the
Red, White and Blue.

—Semi-chorus from the Grand
National Allegory and Tableaux of the
Great Rebellion, by J. M. Hager, 1865

"All honor to thee, thou flag of the free, Emblem of sweet liberty."

"BETSY ROSS" PERFUMED SOUVENIR

BE PATRIOTIC AND USE AMERICA'S BEST PERFUMES

FOR SALE BY YOUR DRUGGIST

Three Patriots

When I see you dear,
I see red, white, and blue dear.
Ev'rybody knows your lips are red
And your cheeks are rosy, too.
Your teeth are bright, they're pearly white
And both of your eyes are blue.
So I'll be true dear,
To the Red, White, and Blue dear,
And, ev'ry time that you hear me brag
How I love the flag, I mean you too.

—Song lyric, "When I See You, I See Red, White,
and Blue," 1917 Copyright 1917, Mills Music, Inc.,
Copyright renewed. Used with permission.
All rights reserved.

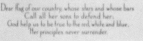

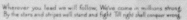

THE GIRL HE LEFT BEHIND

The bugle sounded clear, the parting hour was near,
Her soldier lad must go;
He kissed her goodbye, then, with a sigh,
He marched to meet the foe.

—Song lyric, "How Can I Bear to Leave Thee," by Felix F. Feist, 1906

AMERICA HERE'S MY BOY

THE SENTIMENT OF EVERY AMERICAN MOTHER

I'll fight for you and the Stars and Stri...

WORTH WHILE FIGHTING FOR
TO MAKE THE WORLD SAFE FOR YO...

WORDS BY
ANDREW B. STERLING

JOE MORRIS MUSIC CO.
145 W. 45TH St.   NEW YORK

MUSIC BY
ARTHUR LANGE

GUARDIAN SPIRITS

You are near to my heart and dear to me
And this are old Stars and Stripes

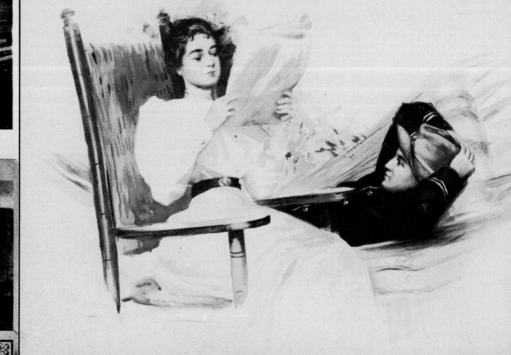

Love to my Soldier Boy.

WE'LL DO OUR SHARE
WHILE YOU'RE OVER THERE

WOMEN!
HELP AMERICA'S SONS
WIN THE WAR

BUY
U.S. GOVERNMENT BONDS
2ND LIBERTY LOAN
OF 1917

JUST A BABY'S PRAYER AT TWILIGHT
(FOR HER DADDY OVER THERE)

WORDS BY
SAM M. LEWIS & JOE YOUNG
MUSIC BY
M. K. JEROME

A Mother's Prayer
for Her Boy Out There

WORDS BY
ANDREW B.
STERLING

MUSIC BY
ARTHUR
LANGE

JOE MORRIS MUSIC CO.   145 W. 45ᵗʰ ST.   NEW YORK

"Heard from him?"
No, not in many a year;
But a mother's a mother,
I s'pose you know,—

Always a hope in
her heart of hearts,
Under the worry and wear of life,
Always a prayer
for the absent one,
That keeps him safe
in the din an' strife.

Always a yearning
to clasp the hand
Of the one that wanders far away;
Though many are safe
in the dear home-fold,
It counts but little
with one astray.

—Mary E. Morrison, "Mother's Boy," 1901

over here,
ou're over there,
nd ev'ry night
say this prayer;
hough I cannot be there
o bear your
oubles and care,
hope you'll do your share.
will comfort me so,
ou'll always be
y baby to me.
dreams I seem to see
ou back on my knee.
ou know the
ct'ry must be won
nd it's up to you, my son.
e'll do our share
hile you're over there.

—Song lyric, "We'll Do Our Share," 1918

Same girl...Same smile...Same cigarette

Back to the Pie

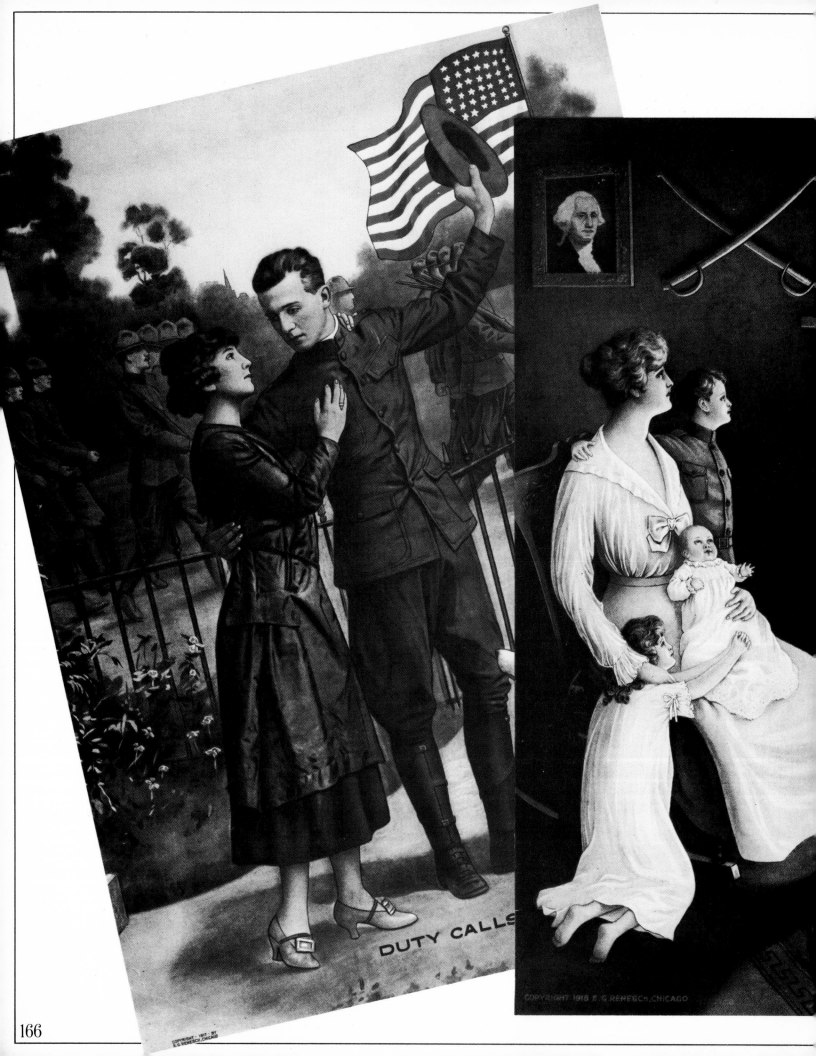

DUTY CALLS

DADDY

ER'S RETURN

MAIDENS IN UNIFORM

Oh, aren't we cute and snappy
in our cover-alls and slacks?
And since the tags say "Sanforized"
we'll stay as cute as tacks!

—Advertisement, "Sanforized," 1942

WHEN I SEE YOU

I SEE RED WHITE AND BLUE

Words by
Grant Clark
Music by
Archie Gottler

Chesterfield

They Rate the Best

A HIGH HONOR FOR YOUR DAUGHTER

THE NAZIS look upon us as a degenerate nation. But they have a great respect for our accomplishments. And, if they win, they may decide that we have something in our blood which they can use in building their master race.

For they're great believers in eugenics, these Nazis. They're strong for selective breeding.

You they may cast aside and put to some ignominious task, such as scrubbing the sidewalks or sweeping the streets. But your daughter...well, if she's young and healthy and strong, a Gauleiter with an eye for beauty may decide she is a perfect specimen for one of their experimental camps.

A high honor for your daughter...

Does this seem a story spun in the realm of fantasy? It isn't. It is now happening, all through

Europe. The latest experiment of the victorious Nazis has been to ship Austrian and Hungarian girls to the Northern countries. The result of these unions...unblessed, of course, by matrimony...will not be known for some time. But the Nazis, you must admit, are not above innovation.

Two, three, four, five years from now they may ship American girls to some far corner of the earth ...may select your daughter...if you relax, if you fail to do your part now. If you say, hopefully, "It can't happen here. We can't lose."

No, we can't lose. We can't afford to. We must not. Else all the terrors, all the degradation, all the misery and suffering that have been loosed upon Europe will be loosed upon us. We of all people will not escape it. We shall be the chosen...we

shall be the elect...in the Nazi scheme of things.

We who have only just begun to win. We who risk the danger of resting on our new-won laurels and considering the job done.

This is no time to relax. This is the time...the opportune time...to do all we can to get this war over sooner.

We *must* measure up to the job!

AMERICAN LOCOMOTIVE

30 CHURCH ST., NEW YORK, N. Y. · MANUFACTURERS OF TANKS · GUN CARRIAGES · ARMY AND NAVY ORDNANCE · STEAM AND DIESEL LOCOMOTIVES

"HIS ONLY SON"

HUMANITY
MARCH

Out of the heavenly splendor,
Down to the trail of woe,
God in his mercy has sent her,
Cheering the world below; —
We call her "Rose of Heaven,"
We've learned to love her so.

There's a rose that grows
On "No Man's Land"
And it's wonderful to see,
Though it's sprayed with tears,
It will live for years,
In my garden of memory…

REPAIRING A MAN OF WAR

Service of All Mankind

JOIN!

The Greatest Mother

...It's the one red rose
The soldier knows,
It's the work of the Master's hand;
'Mid the war's great curse,
Stands the Red Cross Nurse,
She's the rose of "No Man's Land."

Join

YOUR RED CROSS NEEDS YOU

OK - Miss America!
We thank you for your patronage

PICTURE IDENTIFICATION

Definitions

Advertising Card: A small, sometimes lavishly illustrated card bearing a message from the advertiser, and given away to customers by retail tradesmen or storekeepers. These cards were popular in America from 1875 to 1895.

Cabinet Photograph: A form of early photograph used especially for portraiture; cabinet size is 4½" x 6½." The pictures are mounted and bear the imprint of the photographic studio.

Carte de Visite: A commercially produced photographic card, measuring 2½" x 4", sold in stores during the 1860s and 1870s much as postcards are today. Cartes de visite were used as souvenirs and for collecting.

Chromolithograph: A vividly colored lithographic print obtained by using a series of stone plates with different portions of the picture drawn upon them, inked, and superimposed during printing in such a manner that the resulting image appears in full color.

Decorative Print: A chromolithographic print intended for framing.

Die-Cut: A pre-cut shape; a printed decoration generally used for making greetings.

Display Advertisement: A large cardboard advertisement intended for store use, to be displayed on counters or in store windows.

Insert: An illustrated card packed with or inserted in a packaged product and sold to customers in order to persuade them to continue buying the same brand. These cards were commonly sold with tobacco, coffee, and thread during the 1880s and 1890s.

Paper Decorations, Paper Dolls, and Paper Fans: These were among the numerous paper novelties produced in the 1890s and used as advertising or insert cards.

Postcard: A card made specifically for mailing. Postcards were popular in America from 1904 to about 1914 and were revived again, after a near absence, in the late 1930s.

Rotogravure: A picture printed on a rotary press using copper cylinders etched from photographic plates. These pictures generally appeared in a newspaper pictorial section.

Stereograph: A double photograph, usually measuring 3½" x 7", for use with a stereopticon or magic lantern. Stereographs were most popular in America from 1860 to 1890, when nearly all photographers made stereo negatives.

Baking Powder, painted by Maud
Fangel
19. First row
1919 magazine advertisement, Karo
Syrup, probably painted by J. C.
Leyendecker
Second row
1895 Keystone stereograph, "Shaving
Jack"
1920s booklet, Post Toasties
1903 magazine advertisement,
Packer's Tar Soap
20. 1916 writing tablet cover, "School
Days," painted by P. Stanfanos
21. First row
1908 magazine advertisement,
Pearline
1914 postcard
1896 magazine advertisement, Rigby
Process Capes and Jackets
Second row
1906 postcard, "University Series"
1908 postcard
1906 postcard, "University Series"
Third row
1906 postcard, painted by Earl
Christy
1906 magazine advertisement, Hinds'
Cream
1906 postcard, painted by Earl
Christy
22. 1940 rotogravure cover, "The Wearing
of the Green," Picture Parade section
of The Philadelphia Inquirer.
Reprinted by permission
23. Background picture
1919 music cover, "Land of My
Dreams," painted by Haskell Coffin
First row
1944 ink blotter, painted by Earl
Moran. Reprinted by permission
1923 magazine advertisement,
Kimberly-Clark Corporation.
Reprinted by permission
Second row
1908 magazine advertisement,
Pearline
Third row
1907 decorative print, painted by
Harrison Fisher
24. First row
1903 music cover, "The College Girl"
Second row
1908 postcard
1928 Colliers magazine cover, painted
by Edward Irving Valentine
Third row
1890s embossed greeting card
1907 magazine advertisement,
Pearline
1940 magazine advertisement,
Chesterfields. Reprinted by
permission
25. 1905 Booklovers magazine cover

GOOD GIRLS/BAD GIRLS

27. Left
1905 postcard, "Easter"
Right
1909 postcard
30. Left
1902 photographic postcard
Right
1908 postcard
31. First row
1911 postcard

1917 music cover, "Are You from
Heaven?"
Second row
1879 advertising card, Magic Yeast
Cakes
1900 decorative print
1899 cabinet photograph
Third row
1905 postcard, "Hope"
1909 postcard, "Jesu, My Lord"
1908 postcard, "Faith"
32. 1905 Ladies' Home Journal
illustrated editorial, "Composite
Madonna," painted by Joseph Gray
Kitchell, 1900
33. Background picture
1910 poster, Beacon Lights
First row
1904 greeting card
1909 photographic greeting card
Second row
1905 photographic greeting card
1908 photographic greeting card
1909 greeting card
34. 1907 photographic postcard,
hand-colored
35. First row
1907 postcard
1905 photographic postcard, "Gertie
Millar"
1906 magazine advertisement, Pears'
Soap
Second row
1914 postcard, Courtesy of Drew
Eliot
1910 postcard
Third row
1900s stereograph, "Cool and
Contented"
1907 postcard, "Ring Me Up
Sometime"
1906 magazine advertisement, Pears'
Soap
36. First row
1906 magazine advertisement,
Rubifoam for the Teeth
1920s bridge tally card

Second row
1910 photographic postcard
1902 calendar print, New Amsterdam
Theatre, "Dottie Wang." Courtesy
of Gene Szafran
Third row
1889 advertising card, "My Name Is
Hylo"
1905 photographic postcard
1883 advertising card, Samuel Mars
Fine Cigars
37. Background picture
1918 calendar print, "Hello"
First row
1911 postcard
Second row
1907 postcard
38. First row
1939 calendar print, painted by Gil
Elvgren
1941 game board, "Glamor Gal"
1905 photographic postcard
Second row
1909 photographic postcard
Third row
1943 calender print, "Tailwind,"
painted by Gil Elvgren
1908 postcard, "The Wurst Girl"
1920s Valentine greeting

39. First row
1910 photographic postcard.
Courtesy of Drew Eliot
1940s postcard, painted by Earl
Moran. Reprinted by permission
1911 photographic postcard
Second row
1916 photographic postcard.
Courtesy of Yesterday, N.Y.C.
1911 postcard
Third row
1907 postcard
1940s calendar print, "Out of Control,"
painted by Art Frahm
40. 1931 music cover, "Do the New York,"
painted by Alberto Vargas. Reprinted
by permission
41. First row
1886 Gypsy Queen tobacco insert
1901 postcard, "His Affinity."
Courtesy of Drew Eliot
1888 Old Judge tobacco insert
Second row
1870s Sweet Caporal tobacco insert,
"Mabel Clark"
1880s cigarette insert, "Alberta
Gallatin"
Third row
1909 postcard, "The Merry Widow"
1904 postcard. Courtesy of Drew
Eliot
1880s advertising card
Fourth row
1896 cabinet photograph, Haymarket
Theatre, Chicago
1880s cigarette insert, "Josie Sadler"
1880s cigarette insert, "Hope
Latham"
1938 framed calendar picture
1880s cigarette insert, "Stella
Mayhew"
1909 postcard, "A Good Pair to Draw
To"
42-43. Background picture
1902 calendar print, "Beauty and the
Beast." Courtesy of Gene Szafran
First row
1902 photographic postcard, "Beauty
and the Beast," posed by Evelyn
Nesbit
Second row
1904 postcard, "Beauty and the
Beast"
1914 photographic postcard,
hand-tinted
1914 photographic postcard,
hand-tinted

FUN AND FROLIC

45. 1878 chromolithograph
48. 1905 photographic postcard
49. First row
1912 photographic postcard
1912 photographic postcard
Second row
1879 greeting card
1923 Life magazine cover, "Easter,"
painted by Maxfield Parrish.
Reprinted by permission
1879 greeting card
Third row
1910 calendar print, "Floating"
1880s advertising card, Ayer's
Sarsaparilla
1901 cabinet photograph
50. 1924 display advertisement, Outdoor

Girl Rouge. Courtesy of Smolin
Graphic Memorabilia, N.Y.C.
51. First row
1914 postcard
1920s postcard, Monroe Motor
Company
Second row
1930s calendar print
1900s advertising card
1911 magazine advertisement, Baker
Electrics
Third row
1908 greeting card
1908 postcard, "Aunt Betsy Holmes
and Her Horseless Carriage,
Raleigh, N.C."
Fourth row
1905 magazine advertisement, The
Waverly Electric
1912 magazine advertisement, The
Waverly Electric
1905 magazine advertisement, The
Waverly Electric
52-53. First row
1920s magazine advertisement,
Bradley swim suits
1906 postcard
1910 postcard, "Play Ball,"
hand-colored
1906 postcard
1906 postcard
1906 postcard
1910 postcard, Asbury Park, N.J.
Second row
1890s advertising card, Wiggle-Stick
Bluing
1941 Oregon souvenir folder
1900 stereograph, "You Are Not the
Only Pebble on the Beach"
1906 postcard, "I Am Stuck on This
Place"
1924 magazine advertisement,
Palmolive. Reprinted by
permission
Third row
1906 postcard
1906 postcard
1906 postcard, Keansburg, N.H.
1904 postcard, Asbury Park, N.J.
1906 postcard, Put-in-Bay, Ohio,
hand-colored
1906 postcard
Fourth row
1906 postcard
1906 postcard, hand-colored
1906 postcard, "All Alone"
1906 postcard, "Happy as Can Be"
1906 postcard, "Here's Looking at
You"
54. First row
1908 decorative print, "A Trusty
Friend," painted by J. Ross Bryson
1907 postcard, "Autumn Girl," painted
by S. S. Porter
Second row
1890s cigar box label
Third row
1880s advertising card, Ayer's Hair
Renewer
1890s tobacco insert
1910 decorative print, painted by
Howard Chandler Christy
55. First row
1903 postcard, "I'll Catch You"
1940 magazine advertisement,

179

Great Mammy Picture," painted by
W. L. Taylor

AMERICAN BEAUTY

91. 1919 music cover, "My Garden of
Love," painted by Rolf Armstrong

94. 1916 calendar print, "The Prudential
Girl — 1916," painted by Haskell
Coffin. Reprinted by permission

95. First row
1914 postcard
1920 music cover, "Girl of My
Dreams." Reprinted by permission
of the composer, Harry Tobias
1902 postcard, "Dawn," posed by
Evelyn Nesbit
Second row
1902 postcard, "The Debutante,"
posed by Evelyn Nesbit
1898 postcard, "Prudence"
Third row
1917 magazine advertisement,
Pompeian Night Cream

96–97. First row
1900s paper fan, Hosler's Ice Cream
1905 postcard
1911 postcard
1912 postcard
1912 postcard
Second row
1920 magazine advertisement,
Columbia Grafonola, painted by
Gene Pressler
1914 postcard
1911 postcard, painted by Kyra
1920 magazine advertisement,
Columbia Grafonola, painted by
Gene Pressler
Third row
1904 postcard, "Sweet Dreams of
Love"
1884 advertising card, Gale Chilled
Plows
1922 magazine advertisement,
Palmolive. Reprinted by
permission
1904 postcard, "Queen of the Geisha"

98–99. First row
1892 advertising card, Eagle
Cinnamon Wafers
1865 carte de visite, "The Rosebud"
1905 postcard
1905 postcard, "To Woman"
Second row (background)
1916 music cover, "Love Garden"
1898 music cover, "She Was a
Rosebud"
1900 music cover, "Pretty Kitty
Doyle"
Second row (foreground)
1905 postcard
1919 match box cover
1913 postcard
1880 advertising card, "The Yellow
Rose"
1880 greeting card decoration (above)
1906 postcard
Third row
1912 postcard, "Buds"
1905 postcard, "Greeting"
1898 greeting card, "A Merry
Christmas"
1880 greeting card decoration
1901 postcard, "Sincere Wishes"

Fourth row
1905 postcard, "Good Morning"
1907 postcard, "At the Opera,"
painted by Philip Boileau

100. 1926 magazine advertisement,
Madame Jeannette Laboratories

101. First row
1924 magazine advertisement,
Palmolive. Reprinted by
permission
1919 Needlecraft magazine cover
1910 decorative print, painted by
Howard Chandler Christy
Second row
1925 magazine advertisement,
Palmolive. Reprinted by
permission
Third row
1919 magazine advertisement,
Resinol Soap
1916 magazine advertisement,
Canthrox Shampoo
1920s fashion brochure, Shaugnessy

102. 1928 magazine advertisement,
Palmolive

103. First row
1942 magazine advertisement,
Palmolive. Reprinted by
permission
1935 magazine advertisement,
Irresistible Rouge
1914 music cover, posed by Reine
Davies
Second row
1898 decorative print. Courtesy of
Smolin Graphic Memorabilia,
N.Y.C.
1912 Hearst's magazine cover, painted
by Harrison Fisher
1906 advertising card, "Wallacia"
Third row
1922 magazine advertisement,
Sun-Maid Raisins

104. First row
1922 magazine advertisement,
Mulsified Cocoanut Oil Shampoo.
Courtesy of Yesterday, N.Y.C.
1924 magazine advertisement,
Mulsified Cocoanut Oil Shampoo
Second row
1924 magazine advertisement,
Westinghouse. Reprinted by
permission
Third row
1897 magazine advertisement, Hall's
Vegetable Sicilian Hair Renewer
1920 magazine advertisement,
Canthrox Shampoo

105. Background picture
1919 magazine advertisement,
Rubberset Toothbrush
First row
1900 magazine advertisement,
Rubifoam

106. First row
1904 magazine advertisement,
Palmolive
1902 magazine advertisement
Second row
1900 magazine advertisement, Pears'
Soap
1896 magazine advertisement, Pears'
Soap
Third row
1890s cigar box label
1905 magazine advertisement,

Pearline

107. 1924 magazine advertisement,
Listerine

108. First row
1909 magazine advertisement, Royal
Worcester Corset Company
Second row
1880s advertising card, Eureka Health
Corset
1899 stereograph, "Oh! You're a
Peach"
1880s advertising card, Chicago
Corset Company
Third row
1917 magazine advertisement, Ferris
Good Sense Corset
1891 magazine advertisement, Ferris
Bros. Health Corset
1916 magazine advertisement, Kabo
Corset Company

109. 1900 magazine advertisement,
Thomson's Corsets

110. Background picture
1900 magazine advertisement,
American Lady Shoes
First row
1896 advertising card, Candee "Fairy"
Shoes

111. First row
1980s Sensation tobacco insert
1937 magazine advertisement, Arrow
Shirts, painted by Hans Flato.
Reprinted by permission
1890s cabinet photograph. Courtesy
of Bruce Nelson
Second row
1908 postcard, Merry Widow Hats
1909 postcard, "I Can't Kick"
Third row
1905 Ladies' Home Journal editorial
illustration, painted by M.E.
Musselman
1922 photographic postcard
1905 Ladies' Home Journal editorial
illustration, painted by M. E.
Musselman

COURTIN' 'N SPOONIN'

113. 1914 glass slide, advertisement used
in a movie theater

116. 1905 postcard, "Courtship Series"

117. First row
1910 postcard
1910s postcard, Nylo Chocolates
1909 postcard
Second row
1909 postcard
1910 postcard
1920s photographic postcard,
hand-colored
Third row
1909 postcard
1910s photographic postcard,
hand-colored
1914 postcard

118. Background picture
1920 music cover, painted by
Frederick Manning. Courtesy of
Yesterday, N.Y.C.
First row
1909 postcard, "Life Series"
Second row
1911 postcard. Courtesy of Bruce
Nelson
Third row
1908 postcard, "Soldier Series"

119. First row
1909 postcard
1911 postcard. Courtesy of Bruce
Nelson
Second row
1910 postcard
1909 photographic postcard
1907 postcard, "Branding," "Cowboy
Series"
Third row
1909 postcard
1911 postcard
1911 postcard

120–121. 1907 decorative print,
"Alternating Currents," painted by
Howard Chandler Christy

122. 1933 magazine advertisement, The
American Tobacco Company

123. First row
1911 postcard
1911 postcard
1909 postcard
Second row
1912 postcard
1927 magazine advertisement,
Oneida Ltd. Reprinted by
permission
1910 postcard
Third row
1905 postcard, painted by Sydney
Carter
1913 Judge magazine cover, "Speak
for It," painted by James
Montgomery Flagg. Reprinted by
permission

124. First row
1932 magazine advertisement, The
American Tobacco Company,
"Forever and Ever...," painted by
Howard Chandler Christy
Second row
1908 postcard
1910 postcard, "Ring Series"

125. 1911 postcard

126–127. First row
1943 magazine advertisement, Lane
Cedar Hope Chest
1926 magazine advertisement,
Jeannette Cordet Beauty Products
1920 magazine advertisement,
Pompeian Beauty Powder
Second row
1915 magazine advertisement,
Sunkist
1927 magazine advertisement,
Oneida Ltd. Reprinted by
permission
Third row
1941 magazine advertisement,
Oneida Ltd. Reprinted by
permission
1886 music cover, "The Orange
Blossom Bridal Song"
1865 carte de visite, "The Bride"
1940 magazine advertisement,
Oneida Ltd. Reprinted by
permission

128. First row
1907 postcard
1919 magazine advertisement, Life
Savers Candy Mints
Second row
1907 postcard
1911 Ladies' Home Journal magazine
cover, painted by Harrison Fisher.
Reprinted by permission

WOMAN FOREVER
LIBERTY
EQUALITY
MARCH
WOMAN FOREVER
"RESPECTFULLY INSCRIBED TO
WOMANHOOD OF THE UNIVERSE
JUSTICE
LIBERTY
LIBERTY
VICTORY
EQUALITY
EQUALITY
JUSTICE
JUSTICE
VICTORY
BY E.T. PAULL
PUBLISHED BY E.T. PAULL MUSIC Co. 243 WEST 42nd ST.
NEW YORK
PRICE
50¢
LONDON, ENG.
B. FELDMAN.
SPRINGFIELD. MASS.
A. H. GOETTING.
BERLIN, GERMANY,
C. M. ROEHR.
NEW YORK
CROWN MUSIC CO.
NEW YORK
ENTERPRISE MUSIC CO.
NEW YORK.
PLAZA MUSIC CO.
CHICAGO, ILL.
F. J. A. FORSTER CO.
TORONTO, CANADA.
W. R. DRAPER.
Copyright
MCMXVI.
By E.T. PAULL
J. A. ALBERT & SON, SYDNEY, AUSTRALIA.
COPYRIGHT FOR ALL COUNTRIES.
LITH BY A.HOEN & CO. RICHMOND, VA.